# REIGN OF THE EMPRESS 1912 – 2012

## A HISTORY OF THE EMPRESS THEATRE,

## FORT MACLEOD, ALBERTA

Peter J. Scott

William T. Williams, Architect, 1911
Town of Fort Macleod Archives,
Empress Theatre Collection

Empress Theatre Society
P.O. Box 99
235 24 Street
Fort Macleod, Alberta  T0L 0Z0
www.empresstheatre.ab.ca


**Library and Archives Canada Cataloguing in Publication**


**Scott, Peter J., 1949-**
     **Reign of the Empress, 1912-2012 : a history of the Empress Theatre, Fort Macleod, Alberta / Peter James Scott.**


**Includes bibliographical references and index.**
**ISBN 978-0-9880332-0-7**


     **1. Empress Theatre (Fort Macleod, Alta.)--History.**
**2. Theaters--Alberta--Fort Macleod--History.  3. Fort Macleod (Alta.)--Buildings, structures, etc.  I. Title.**


**FC3699.F67Z57 2012     725'.8220971234     C2012-902556-9**


*project committee:* Bonnie Kennedy, Gary Kennedy, Mary Oordt, Martin Oordt, Judy Stetson
*cover and interior design:* Karen Alm, Just Call Marketing & Graphics
*front cover photo:* Jaime Vedres Photography


Printed in Canada by The Warwick Printing Co. Ltd. on partially recycled paper using vegetable oil based inks.

# DEDICATION

This book is dedicated to the people of Fort Macleod and area who, be they patrons, benefactors, visionaries, performers or romantics, have kept memories of the Empress Theatre – and their own – alive for 100 years.

# CONTENTS

## FOREWORD
### BY JIM MOUNTAIN

"YEARS AGO, people from miles around came into town on a Saturday night, dressed up fine, and went to the show at the Empress. Then, around 10 o'clock they'd promenade out onto Main Street and into the stores and restaurants opened for shopping. Some would stay open until after midnight until the last of them left..." So stated Charlie Edgar, former Fort Macleod mayor and amazing raconteur, who would come into the Main Street project office almost daily to tell our Main Street staff stories of the town's past. His anecdotes helped fuel the efforts to preserve the Empress and other buildings in Macleod's historic downtown.

In the early 1980s the Empress's doors were open, but barely. The theatre was operated by owners who lived out of town. Theatregoers drove to Lethbridge to see first-run movies that the Empress could not book. To add insult to injury, some would reportedly stop at the Empress to buy their popcorn on a Friday or Saturday night, before heading out to shows in the city.

The Empress was in danger of becoming outmoded and potentially suffering the fate of hundreds of theatres across Canada and the United States. In the emerging age of video rentals, cable and satellite television and multiplex theatres, old-time theatres were being demolished or converted to other commercial uses. The Empress was not quite there yet, and remarkably, her fate was about to be decided.

In 1982, the Empress was calling out for love and attention. One could imagine her 1940s glory when first gazing up at the lit neon tulips on the pressed-tin ceiling. The graffiti on the wooden walls in the small dressing rooms downstairs gave a wonderful hint as to whom had performed there from 1912 onward. The two person "love-seats" spoke of romance and of couples gazing in awe at Hollywood's stars on the big screen. The Empress offered a few hours respite for trainees at the Commonwealth Air Training base from the thoughts of going overseas to that much bigger reality show, the theatre of the Second World War.

In the 1980s the building seriously needed help. Water was seeping through one wall, discharged from a dry-cleaning business next door. The stage was literally used as a storage space, buried in boxes, old vending machines and miscellaneous junk. The movie screen was tacked onto the front of the stage, reducing its depth and making live performances impossible. Seat upholstery was tired and worn. The floors were caked with generations of spilled drinks and trodden-in bubble gum. But one could see that she was a true gem beneath the veneer of wear and tear.

Thankfully, several positive initiatives were championed by people who believed that the future of the town meant, in large measure, the respecting of its past. People such as Mayor Wes Olmstead and Council; Hugh Craig and the business community; the Fort Museum; the Fort Players and Sebastian David; Alberta Culture; Historic Sites Service;

the Heritage Canada Foundation chaired by writer Pierre Berton and yes, the private owners of the theatre, one in Calgary and one in Toronto, who listened and allowed access to the building. Somehow all of these people got behind the concept of preserving Fort Macleod's downtown area, of which the Empress occupied a prominent space.

Small steps started the Empress turn-around. The town applied and was accepted into Heritage Canada Foundation's Main Street program. This project focused on reviving historic downtowns, mainly by getting as many people as possible working together for the overall economic, social and cultural well-being of the community. A store-front project office was established on Main Street. Serving several purposes, the office became the first booking and promotion centre for the reviving of the Empress Theatre. A dinner at Fort Player's Sebastian and Eva David's house with the Empress owners opened the doors to community use. The junk was cleared off the stage. The movie screen was re-positioned to the back wall, thus freeing up the stage for programming.

The strategy of "more is better" made risks to be taken on blind faith that programming live performances at the Empress would bring in people and build support for her preservation. Musician friends from the Lethbridge Folk Club, including Macleod's Maureen Chambers, gave their time to perform for the Alberta minister of culture, town council and residents. The University of Lethbridge Drama department's Brian Parkinson got involved in 1983 as mentor to 10 drama students. They formed the summer theatre troupe Great West Theatre performing vintage melodramas, with two shows daily at the impossible times of 10 a.m. and 3 p.m.

The show "A Sentimental Evening" with the Lethbridge Big Band to commemorate the Commonwealth Air Training Plan, sold out the Empress on a winter's night with some Second World War veterans attending in their original uniforms. It was an emotional night filled with warmth. A couple who had met at the Empress during those war years travelled from Calgary some 40 years later and received a standing ovation from all. The matinee Christmas movie, shown after the first Santa Claus Parade organized by the Main Street office, saw the Empress resonate with the laughter of children again.

Huge credit must go to Main Street manager Louise Heric, project architect Art Ferrari and the Fort Macleod Historic Area committee for taking the Empress restoration to the next level. The town's intense lobbying to the province brought in the much-needed investment to enable the Empress to be purchased and restored to the top-quality dual film and live theatre venue it is today. That investment arguably has paid immeasurable quality of life dividends. The Empress has literally put Fort Macleod on Canada's national cultural map. The ambience and continued excellent programming at the Empress has enriched and delighted southern Albertans and visitors to the region.

It took people with vision and belief in Fort Macleod to build and operate the Empress

100 years ago. In those heady years in Alberta just two years before the First World War, constructing this theatre signalled a sense of permanence and ambition. For a century now, it's taken a succession of people with equal vision and commitment to keep the doors open, to enable thousands of residents and visitors to enjoy magical performances on the Empress' stage and screen.

As the British playwright and actor Noel Coward stated: "the theatre should be treated with respect. The theatre is a wonderful place, a house of enchantment, a temple of illusion." The Empress is truly enchanting as the jewel on Main Street. Peter Scott's wonderful history of the Empress captures the essence of the theatre and those people who have dedicated countless hours and years in support of this place of creativity and wonder.

As Charles Dickens wrote: "there's nothing in the world equal to seeing the house rise at you, one sea of delightful faces, one hurrah of applause!" May the delightful faces rise at the Empress for generations to come, the walls resounding with applause as they have since 1912.

Jim Mountain
Ottawa, Ontario
November 2011

Jim Mountain co-ordinated Heritage Canada Foundation's pilot Main Street Canada project in Fort Macleod, Alberta, 1982-1984. From this experience, he established Main Street Canada projects in towns and cities from Manitoba to British Columbia, the Yukon and the Northwest Territories. Today, he works as a planner with the City of Ottawa's Arts and Heritage Unit

# NOTES AND ACKNOWLEDGEMENTS

FOR THE LAST CENTURY, the story of the Empress Theatre has been played out in lockstep with the story of Fort Macleod and its people.

The Empress was built to entertain the town's citizens at a time when fortune and great enterprise was within their grasp, when economic triumph was something on which a man would bet the farm. But forces unforeseen were still at play. The industrial picture of southern Alberta had yet to gel, and the volatile vagaries of commerce ultimately deigned the bounty would settle elsewhere.

At that point, the Empress could have proven to be a fair-weather friend, opened for a dollar and closed on a dime. Instead, the theatre has been a steadfast pillar of the town, sometimes down at heel, often neglected, rarely forgotten. Today, the Empress plays a vibrant role in the community, both as a house of entertainment, as an attraction for tourists, and as keeper of community memories.

In writing *Reign of the Empress*, I have attempted to resurrect in a few short pages the atmosphere surrounding the theatre project in 1912 and to describe how time and tide affected the building throughout the next 10 decades. If I have succeeded, I did so only through the guidance and assistance of several people who showed me around corners, behind curtains and under floor boards.

Chief among those who served as interpreter of the past was Bonnie Kennedy, long an Empress patron, who started as a rich mine of information, became an editor and valued critic and wound up a friend. A writer herself, Bonnie could have put together this book on her own; at times I merely served as her sorcerer's apprentice with a hard drive and keyboard. The rest of the Empress Theatre Society Centennial Book Committee (Gary Kennedy, Mary Oordt and Judy Stetson) also provided valuable advice, as did Marty Oordt until his passing in the spring of 2011.

People interviewed for this book met with me in the town library (Darrel and Flory Fraser), the *Macleod Gazette* office (Sharon Monical, Louise Heric), Rahn's Bakery (Brent Hutchinson, Denise Calderwood), the Empress basement (Al Park), and in the theatre proper (Dennis James, Sharon Hellman, Ryland Moranz.) Others invited me into their homes with scrapbooks and photo albums on kitchen tables displaying pages of pride (Sebastian David, Daisy Young, Bob and Ken Hart, Mary Ruller and family, and Delle Schmidt). Some even allowed me to abscond with their memorabilia, an act of trust I fully appreciate. Juran Greene, Elizabeth Songer, the late Art Ferrari and Edith Becker took time from their professional hours to share their expertise and Empress experiences. David Coutts, Jim Mountain, Wes Olmstead and Shawn Patience spoke eloquently about the Empress, and Betty Boyle shared her reminiscences of her late husband Neil, by telephone and email.

One writer who went before me in describing a special era of Empress history deserves my profound appreciation. Mary Yvonne Dunne, daughter of former owner Dan Boyle, forwarded to me her unpublished manuscript, one in which she has meticulously detailed her memories of her family's time with the Empress. In it, she shared with me – and, in turn, I share them here with readers – invaluable letters written by her loquacious father, who, in corresponding with his betrothed, Edna Swanson, manages to describe the running of a small-town theatre in a few pages better than any book can hope to.

Much of the research for *Reign of the Empress* was placed at my fingertips in a publication by Marselle Jobs Thompson, a veteran of two Great West Theatre summers, who, in a 1990 thesis for her masters of arts, did much of the heavy archival digging, saving me from countless hours either chained in grim newspaper vaults or stuck before a microfiche reader. Of course, those newspapermen of long-ago Fort Macleod, reporters for the *Advertiser, Gazette, News, Spectator* and *Times*, all receive posthumous praise for their intriguing descriptions of the community's life which appear here.

Readers will note the "Fort" in the town's name appears to disappear and reappear. This is historically accurate: the community was known as Fort Macleod from 1874 until it was incorporated as Macleod in 1892. It was restored to Fort Macleod in 1953, in part to reflect its history.

In a few instances, primarily during the early days of the Empress, I have taken the liberty of fictionalizing the thoughts of some of the key characters responsible for her birth and early care. While merely my invention, their ruminations on the circumstances in which they find themselves is based on the realities of the day and, hopefully, creates context for the reader.

Peter J. Scott
Lethbridge, Alberta
November 2011

CHAPTER ONE

# UNDER NEON TULIPS AND ALBERTA SKIES

FORT MACLEOD, Alberta, August 2011. In the noon heat of a southern Alberta summer, the Empress Theatre begins to empty out. The year's keen attendees at summer drama camp are scrambling to locate lunch bags, arrange drinks, and, with a little coaxing, herd orderly out of the theatre's cool basement into the blast furnace of Main Street in search of a shady locale to enjoy a deserved repast after a morning of painting scenery.

Like most children, they live in and for the moment. Their conversation swirls between idle babble and serious discussion of their morning progress. Far from their minds, on this glorious summer day, is any contemplation that the old theatre – their theatre – will mark its centenary in a few short months.

The youngest appear to be about 10, making them toddlers the last time the Empress celebrated a decade: its ninetieth birthday in 2002. It's likely, if they are the progeny of long-time Fort Macleod citizenry, their great-grandparents once elbowed their way through the same doors, rushing eagerly into the labyrinth of another Saturday celluloid adventure, and then back out shielding their eyes from the same summer sunlight after an afternoon of flying bullets, blood-curdling monsters and general matinee mayhem. Perhaps a relative once performed here as an actor or musician, ushered customers to their rows and seats ("BB4 is in the balcony, ma'am") or swept spilled popcorn from aisles following shows. If so, it would be no surprise to anyone in town. The Empress Theatre has become the town's generational time warp, a cornerstone of its history.

The Empress was here to help the town celebrate its days of wild early optimism and, when the parade of commercial growth opted for a different route, to strike up the band to fill the disappointed silence. When crops failed and the land was stripped bare during the Depression, the theatre managed to scratch up enough joy to replant and nourish the faith that drew people here in the first place. The Empress was here to give rousing send-offs to Commonwealth flyers training for Europe's aerial battlegrounds and present newsreels of the war to those who kept the fires burning at home. The theatre remained a solid citizen, waiting patiently for the community to rediscover its direction and later, when Fort Macleod determined its past was, in fact, its future, the Empress proudly assumed its pride of place, a saucy flourish of red brick shouldered amid its sombre greystone contemporaries on Main Street.

The Empress has been a showpiece and a showplace for 100 years, a site of a prairie town's renaissance in all forms of entertainment. Today, amid the skittering children heading for the outdoors, the Empress has added a new role to its repertoire, providing educational opportunities to learn about theatrical endeavours and music of all genres.

This season's students scurry into the sunshine, their voices soon blending with the noise of street traffic as the theatre's paned doors swing shut behind them. As young thespians, perhaps they, too, will make the journey from a childhood summer activity in the basement to a spotlighted evening on the Empress stage. Regardless, they are creating their own memories of the theatre as generations of southern Albertans have for a century. "Southern Albertans," because although the Empress is inarguably a Fort Macleod landmark, it has been a destination for folks from throughout the region who have laughed, tapped toes, applauded and been entertained by its performers since it opened in 1912.

On that opening day, Canada turned 45, while Alberta, a mere sprout among provinces, was seven. Manitoba, Ontario and Quebec expanded their boundaries to 60 degrees north. Newfoundland was a British colony. When the year began, there were but 46 united states in the union, two world wars were yet to be fought (although the Balkans started their own dust-up later that year), and the *Titanic* was still unsinkable, at least until mid-April. The year 1912 is noted for the first parachute jump from an aircraft, the first Calgary Stampede and the second Indianapolis 500. A day before the Empress opened, a tornado touched down in Regina, killing 28 citizens and destroying much of the city's downtown; known as the Regina Cyclone, it was actually a tornado, still the deadliest in Canadian history. On a more theatrical note, Universal Pictures was founded in Hollywood, and in the Empress concession, patrons might have purchased 1912's new rolled candy, the Lifesaver.

In Macleod, with a population roughly what it is today, the Empress, built as part of the Famous Players chain, was but one of three sites in which citizens could enjoy a movie; more accurately, the Empress was opening as an "opera house," assuming airs to match its royal name. After a few years of opposition, however, the Empress was left to carry on alone, at the same moment a source of community pride, a link to a prosperous past, and a portal for patrons to enjoy first-rate acts in a thriving entertainment industry.

Patrons enjoying the theatre today become a small part of Empress history, joining countless others who have passed through the lobby and back into a time of vaudeville, minstrel shows, or community concerts or watched the march of movie technology from *Wings* to *Star Wars* accompanied by the tinkle of piano or THX surround sound.

Photo: Gary Kennedy

How many date nights began in the red-velvet seats, how many subsequent anniversaries were celebrated with tickets to memorable concerts? How many deserved standing ovations have audiences meted out throughout the first century? How many performers have been loudly hailed back for encores? How many of the artists recorded their appearances on the dressing room walls or counted their Empress experiences as highlights in their careers? Certainly, memories have been made here: hands held, kisses stolen, careers emboldened, winters warmed and summers cooled. The Empress is Fort Macleod's cultural warehouse, in which its history is kept safe and its future waits to be uncrated.

The Empress is Alberta's oldest, continuously operating theatre, a venue, since 1912, for all manner of entertainment serving up most of what could be enjoyed on tap in larger centres on the Canadian prairies. Music, dance, drama, comedy, opera, movies, political rallies, wrestling: all have been part of the rich Empress playbill through its first 100 years. It has survived economic trials and political skirmishes, while two major renovations have succeeded in upgrading and improving the facility preserving, for the most part, its look, feel and history.

No lady enjoys giving away her measurements, but at 100 years old, the Empress is likely beyond those vanities:

Width: 36 feet (11m).

Length: 99 feet (30m).

Floor area: 3,564 square feet (331m²).

Slope of floor: 3 feet (0.9m) from rear to stage.

Ceiling height: 18 feet, 9 inches (5.7m) at the rear;
21 feet, 9 inches (6.6m) at the front.

Beaux-Arts arch: about 15 feet (4.6m) wide and 15 feet (4.6m) high.

Oculus window: 3 feet (0.9m) in diameter.

Lantern, or projection, room: 36 feet (11m) by 13 feet (4.0m).

Auditorium: 36 feet (11m) wide, 72 feet, 8 inches (22.2m) long,
including orchestra pit, but not the stage.

Orchestra pit: 16 feet (4.9m) by 6 feet (1.8m), dropped 12 inches
(30cm) and enclosed by a 24-inch (0.6m) railing.

Stage area: 36 feet (11m) wide and 14 feet (4.3m) deep, raised 4 feet
(1.2m) above the auditorium floor.

Proscenium: 22 feet (6.7m) wide and 15 feet (4.6m) high.

Basement: 972 square feet (90.3m²).

Three dressing rooms: two at 4 feet, 6 inches (1.4m) by 7 feet (2.1m);
one at 6 feet (1.8m) by 7 feet (2.1m).

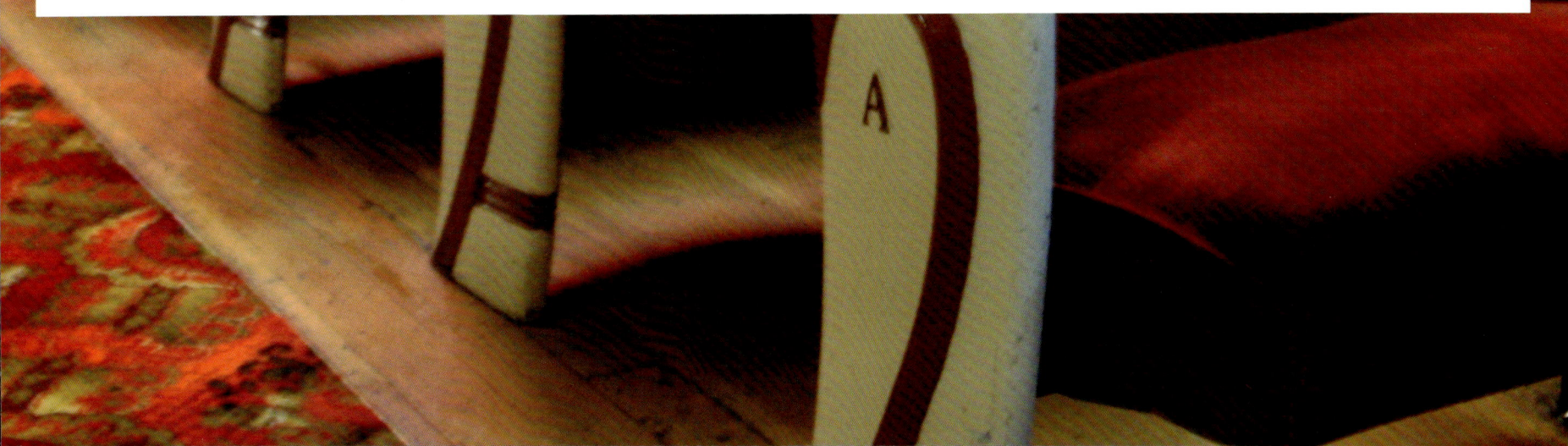

The Empress experience begins before patrons reach the front doors. In the late fall to early spring months, when an 8 p.m. start means darkness has already cloaked Main Street, the theatre marquee and light spilling through the front doors make the Empress the brightest building on the block. Patrons can be found either waiting in line to enter or connecting in curbside conversation, their streetside meetings creating a sense of excitement as show time approaches. Certainly this curbside overflow is due to the tiny Empress lobby and perhaps its no-smoking policy but, regardless, it proves the lure of the Empress does not stop at its entrance.

Once through the paned front doors, visitors are confronted by several options. Dead ahead is the five-sided ticket booth. To the left is the concession counter serving, arguably, southern Alberta's best popcorn. To the right is the stairway to the green room downstairs. Past the booth are two sets of double doors leading to a small corridor running perpendicular to the theatre. From there, two archways lead to the main-floor seats. To the right is a set of eighteen stairs leading to the balcony, taking patrons through 270 degrees to face the front when they arrive at the top.

Entering the auditorium, a visitor's attention is immediately held by two features unique to the Empress: the

Neil Boyle painting of Fay Wray, the heroine in the original *King Kong*.

Neil Boyle painting of Treaty Seven signatories Bull Head, Red Crow and Crowfoot.

Images Courtesy: Betty Boyle

Photo: Gary Kennedy

Theatre seats, Neil Boyle's paintings on the walls and neon tulips on the ceiling.

oft-described trio of neon tulips dominating the main ceiling (there are two more above the balcony) and the six larger-than-life paintings adorning the walls, creations of the late Neil Boyle, whose father, Dan Boyle, owned the Empress for a quarter of its existence. Down the left, from the rear, the artworks depict Treaty Seven signatories Bull Head, Red Crow and Crowfoot; Gilbert M. "Broncho Billy" Anderson, born Maxwell Henry Aronson, an American actor, director, producer, writer and one of the first cowboy movie stars; and American comedian W. C. Fields. On the right are Colonel James Macleod of the Northwest Mounted Police, the artist's father in the ceremonial headdress presented to him as Chief Bull Horn, and Fay Wray the Cardston belle whose best-known role was the heroine in the original *King Kong*.

The main floor seating for 267 is asymmetrical: the centre section contains 17 rows of seven seats each, for 119 seats. Each row contains one "loveseat" at alternating ends, which assists in off-setting the remaining seats. The right side is in line with the main section at the front, but includes two extra rows at the rear. Four seats in each row make for a total of 76 seats. The left side's 18 rows of four seats each begin one row back of the centre section and end in line with the right side, for another 72 seats. The balcony adds 56 seats on the left and 49 on the right, bringing the theatre's capacity to 372. Mere details, perhaps, conveying little of the atmosphere and personality of the Empress but particulars that outline her historic attributes, nevertheless.

From the balcony, seven additional steps lead to the projection booth, a place of dark arts and magic in the eyes of any child seated below waiting for a film to start. Crowded and cluttered, the booth has witnessed changes in projection technology, from death-defying carbon-arc lighting to modern

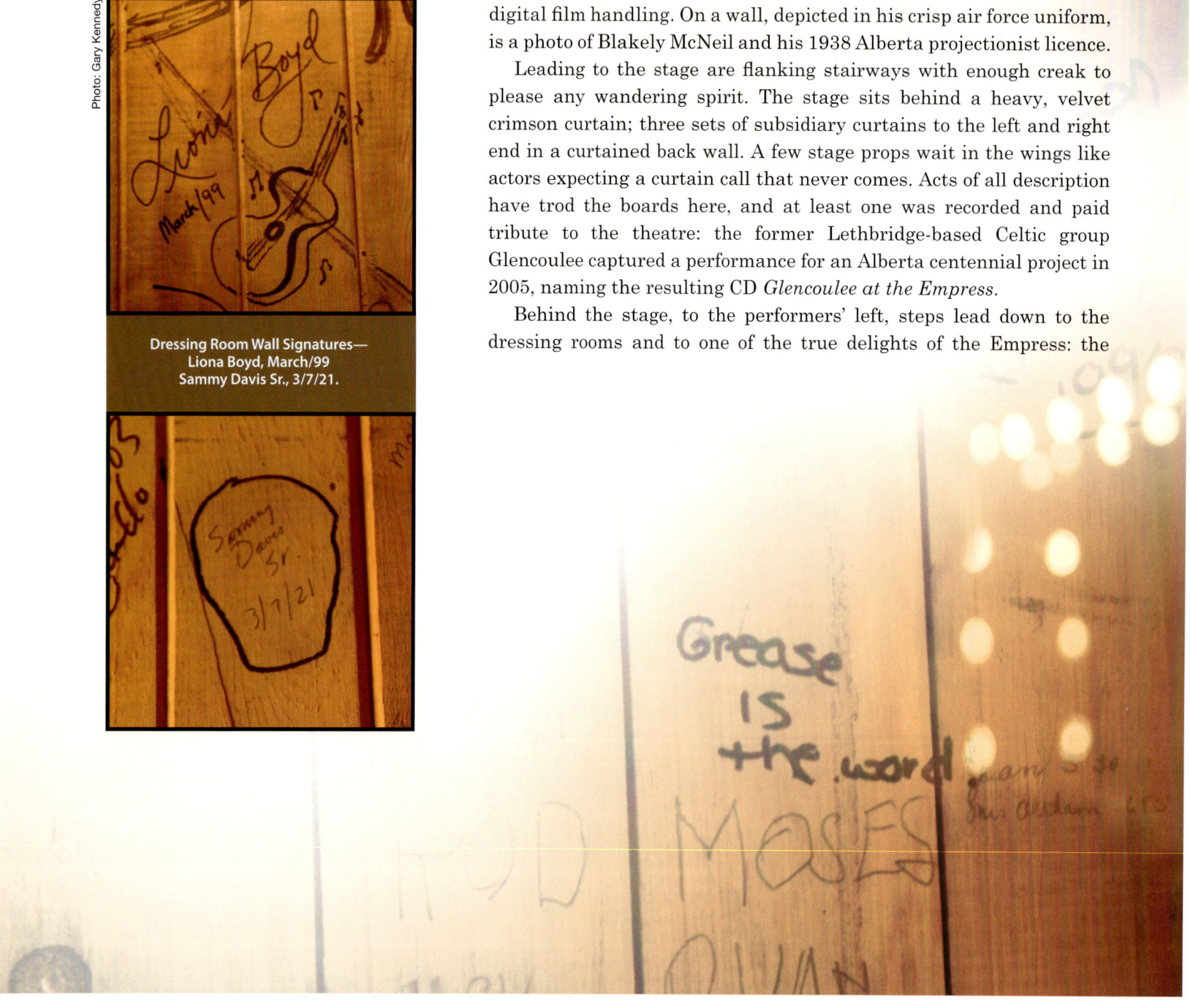

**Dressing Room Wall Signatures—
Liona Boyd, March/99
Sammy Davis Sr., 3/7/21.**

digital film handling. On a wall, depicted in his crisp air force uniform, is a photo of Blakely McNeil and his 1938 Alberta projectionist licence.

Leading to the stage are flanking stairways with enough creak to please any wandering spirit. The stage sits behind a heavy, velvet crimson curtain; three sets of subsidiary curtains to the left and right end in a curtained back wall. A few stage props wait in the wings like actors expecting a curtain call that never comes. Acts of all description have trod the boards here, and at least one was recorded and paid tribute to the theatre: the former Lethbridge-based Celtic group Glencoulee captured a performance for an Alberta centennial project in 2005, naming the resulting CD *Glencoulee at the Empress*.

Behind the stage, to the performers' left, steps lead down to the dressing rooms and to one of the true delights of the Empress: the autographs and graffiti left on the walls during the years by performers of all types and stature. Early ones are written in pencil, later ones in pen and felt marker, while the more industrious signatories (or those with more time on their hands) engraved their names in the red brick. Most names and messages are preserved behind Plexiglas. Perhaps the most intriguing autograph is that of American dance man Sammy Davis who signed as "Sr." in 1921 before the birth of his son Sammy in 1925. Here, too, one finds the name of Trevor Panczak, a southern Albertan country star, inside a heart with Julaine Newton. Liona Boyd left her signature and a drawing of a guitar in March 1999; a decade later, Buffy Sainte Marie signed in. The casts and crews of several stage shows have autographed the walls, including those involved with, among others, *Grease*; *The Lion, The Witch and the Wardrobe*; and *Winnie the Pooh*. American folk singer Kate Wolf wrote a bit of whimsy in April 1985: "Kate Wolf & friends songs from the coast of California under neon tulips and Alberta skies." Sadly, the Empress was part of her final tour; she died at 44, less than two years later after a battle with leukemia. Sarah McLachlan's 1992 wish for the Empress is here: "PEACE LOVE & happiness to you." Randy Bachman left his mark in April 2005. In 2007, Jay & the Americans boldly recommended "Do it loud in FM," while Colin James and Craig Northey signed together that November, both dropping guitar picks behind the Plexiglas. Members of the Arrogant Worms left their mark a year later.

Several posters and advertisements hide downstairs, including this one from July 1919:

> Harvey's Greater Minstrels And Creole Beauty Chorus! Instead of showing you the same threadbare acts you have seen year after year, we spread before you a magnificent multitude of new acts and novelties. Prices 50 cents 75 cents $1. Gay minstrels in gaudy attire.

Here, too, is evidence that in February 1920, to promote an unnamed detective movie, the Empress resorted to the "Mysterious Mr. Raffles" ploy. The same scheme was used in 1907 by the *Los Angeles Times*, which ran teaser photos of the Mysterious Mr. Raffles and offered $1,000 to any reader who spotted him on the street, provided the person had a paid-up, one-year subscription to the newspaper.[1] Two years earlier, to promote a performance in Chicago, an ad declared in large type "The Mysterious Mr. Raffles will attend" with the word "not" in much smaller type inserted after "will".[2] In the Macleod version, the Empress offered, a trifle redundantly, to "give away free" $5 to anyone spotting Raffles on the street and greeting him with the phrase "You are the Mysterious Mr. Raffles." It's unrecorded if anyone won the money.

The three cramped original dressing rooms and a small washroom now open onto a larger dressing room, made possible by renovations to the basement in the 1980s, and ultimately lead to the green room. Here audiences often have the opportunity to meet performers, either at intermissions or after shows, adding a personal Empress-style touch to their evenings.

Back beyond the public area of the green room and dressing rooms is an underground walkway leading under the rear alley to an above-ground storage facility, part of the most recent renovation in 1982. It's another of the nooks and crannies, turns and folds that have become part of the theatre's evolution in its first century, turning from a fine and fancy opera house into a beloved repository of community memories.

An early Macleod newspaper, in announcing plans for the Empress in early 1912, suggested the theatre would become a great addition to the community. One hundred years of proof later, that prediction has been verified and rings true into the theatre's second century.

*JAMES LAMBERT clutched at his coat collar as a defence against the January weather as he strode down Main Street in Fort Macleod, heading from his office one street over toward the Silver Grill restaurant, a warming cup of coffee on his mind. It was also his intent, on this rare break from the daily concerns of his contracting firm, to seek out a copy of the latest* Macleod Advertiser, *published just that day. With business thriving in the burgeoning prairie town, Lambert's time to relax with the newspaper, any newspaper, had been limited of late, a rifling of its few pages the most for which he ever found time.*

*As a conscientious businessman, he would have been checking that day's edition to ensure his ad had been included and printed as per his instructions. As one of several contractors in the thriving prairie town, Lambert was among the most prominent, but it was still prudent to ensure one's name was continuously before the public and spelled correctly, especially in this time of growth and prosperity.*

*There was, of course, a second reason to pique his interest in that particular edition. The* Advertiser *did a reasonable job of informing its readers of developments in Fort Macleod, often in breathless reports sandwiched between dubious advertisements hailing the restorative virtues of the latest elixir, divorce proceedings, estate sales, curling results and fashionable local teas.*

*The item Lambert sought in today's edition was of primary importance. As he ordered his coffee and eased into the cafe's steamy warmth, he found it in the only appropriate place such vital community news could be printed: at the top of page one. As he read, he wondered if Martin had had a chance to read the* Advertiser's *story:*

## CHAPTER TWO
# A FINE NEW OPERA HOUSE

## CONTRACT LET FOR A FINE NEW OPERA HOUSE

To be Built this Year on Twenty-fourth Street for T. B. Martin. Will Seat 500 and be up-to-date in every Particular.

Macleod is to have a new opera house. In every particular except, perhaps size, it will not be surpassed by any in the province. J. S. Lambert has received the contract for its construction and it is anticipated that work will begin as soon as weather permits. The theatre will be erected by T. B. Martin on his lot on Twenty-fourth street just east of Cunningham Bros. hardware store. It will be of brick and stone and practically fireproof and have a seating capacity of 500. The stage will be 14 x 22 feet. The dressing rooms baggage rooms and hot water heater will be in the basement. There will be an orchestra pit and every modern accessory of a first-class theatre.

It will be artistically furnished and decorated and the dome front with plate glass windows on the street, will be a great addition to the appearance of the town's chief thoroughfare.

Mr. Martin is building the opera house which will be leased to a syndicate which controls a circuit of [Famous Players] theatres throughout the West. The front part of the building will be occupied by two offices.

The new opera house will be finished in time for next season's business and then it will be a permanent and joyful farewell to the wretched old Town Hall.

Macleod needs a new theatre. She is going to have it.[1]

## J. S. LAMBERT

### Contractor and Builder

Estimates given on all classes of buildings. First-class work guaranteed.

Picture Mouldings and Fine Wallpapers.

Shop on Twenty-third Street
West of Union Bank

Ad from 1912 issues of *The Macleod Advertiser*—January 23, 30; February 8.

*Pleased with the account, and enjoying the added glow of seeing his name prominent in the piece, Lambert returned to his coffee and gazed at the empty lot just across 24th, a perfect piece of real estate right at the heart of the main thoroughfare. Here he would construct Thomas Martin's theatre once Williams finished the drawings. With luck and a chinook or two before winter's end, he and his crew would have it ready for occupancy by summer, perhaps even as early as June. Then he could turn his attention to the town's new hospital, which he was expected to have completed that summer, too. At 41 beds, balconies for convalescing, extensive lighting and fancy columns, and with Premier Sifton expected for the grand opening, it was a far larger project than*

*the little shoebox theatre to be sure, no matter how grand the name. But a theatre – an "opera house," the* Advertiser *had deemed it – was something special. It would add to the town's cultural doings in a much grander way than the existing Maple Leaf, Majestic or Lyric theatres. With the right building materials, who knew? He couldn't foresee the fate of the buildings, but his hopes were that both the theatre and the hospital might last well into the 1960s, more than half a century.*

*Lambert forced his attention from the frosted windows of the Silver Grill and briefly scanned the rest of the* Advertiser's *front page, barely noting news of the Oddfellows skating party in the "covered rink," or the annual meeting of the Christ Church Parish. He breezed over the small ad for a gramophone and 40 records, priced at $25. He had little time for gramophones and music, considering the work which lay ahead of him. A good Lancashire lad, he had, in his early twenties, emigrated for Canada in 1889 and a chance to see the world. Well, ever since, he had seen plenty of it to be sure, but this little prairie community was now home and no longer a refuge for men escaping their dreary pasts. He had enjoyed his eight years in the Northwest Mounted Police, the Klondike rather less so, although just to be there during the gold rush had been worth the frostbite and near starvation. Those two agents of the devil could kill a man as surely as a Boer's bullet, and he had had enough of those whistle past his head* in South Africa following his Yukon adventure. At least enlisting in the Lord Strathcona Horse had gotten him out of -40 winters, and serving under Sam Steele was an honour in itself. Besides, as a member of the Horse, he had been almost front and centre at the coronation of Edward VII. Imagine, 11 years ago now, and sonny George on the throne for almost two years.

He recalled how, when he left Africa, he tossed around a bit for a place to go next; Macleod had always been in his mind since he left it for the gold fields; thought he might as well give it another go. He wouldn't find gold there, but on the other hand, he'd likely not be shot at, either. Besides, he knew how to use a hammer from his Lancashire boyhood. There was a town to build, money to be made, and he, James Lambert, was making his mark here. He and his wife, Emma Lavinia Taylor, had settled in. Nine years of marriage had blessed them with a daughter and a son and, if their good fortune held, they'd have more. He had worked hard, his business was now prospering. He helped keep some 35 employees and their families out of the poor house, and the buildings he was erecting were changing the face of the community he once helped police. If anyone should be contracted to build this opera house, it was he, and he would greet this unique challenge, an opera house, with customary vigor.

Lambert had seen the craftsmanship employed by Scots stonemasons who used sandstone carted from the Porcupine Hills to build the Queen's Hotel. A quarry at Monarch, 15 miles east, had been operating for a few years, too, and provided stone for the work he had done on the MacDonnell Building in 1909, Andrews Hardware, Anderton Block, Reach's Store, 41 Meats, Horseshoe Liquor Store, Great West

Saddlery, and McNeil-Mathews Block. But Lambert wanted red brick for his Empress. It was tough building brick buildings in this town when one didn't have a quality brickyard close at hand, at least one large enough to produce the number and quality he'd need for the Empress. Sure, these smaller operators could produce soft-mud bricks, but Lambert knew Williams would want to use crisp, well-fired bricks on his theatre, and rightly so. He'd order the bricks maybe from Lethbridge or, even better, Medicine Hat-Redcliff. Many buildings in Alberta were built of brick from that region, and Williams would probably want to use the finest.

Best finish his coffee and march back to the office. He could begin lining up materials and workmen if Williams had sent the plans. It wasn't the easiest of careers, raising a town, city, really, from the bald prairie, but it was a way for a man to leave his mark in the world, that was for sure, even in this small corner of the Dominion of Canada.

Jim Jr., Emma Lavinia, Olive, and Jim (James) Lambert (1909/10).

We can only imagine the thoughts of James Lambert that January day in 1912 as he contemplated building the Empress. The only son of a second marriage, Lambert chose Western Canada as his new home, while several half-siblings settled in the southern United States. The distance between them precluded a close family relationship.[2] Life in Macleod was favourable and it's reasonable to conclude he read the *Advertiser's* article, written in the editorializing and promotional style of the day, and took some pride in being part of the theatre's early beginnings. During his time in Macleod, he served as town councilor, chief of the fire brigade and member of the school board. His granddaughter, Judy Rennie of Toronto, believes Lambert honed his carpentry skills while in the NWMP, so that law enforcement and construction gave him a divided highway to travel for most of what would come later.[3] Could a man enjoy a fuller or more multifaceted life than Lambert, immigrant, frontier cop, gold-rush miner, cavalry officer, soldier in two wars (one of which had yet to break out when he began building the Empress)?

Lambert was, in fact, a busy man in 1912, one of the most productive years in the town's history. He would ultimately build the hospital, the Reach & Co. building, the McDonnell block (adjacent to where he would build the Empress), the White Hall, a school, the arena, several stately Macleod homes and the Bank of Montreal in Lethbridge. He would enjoy a long and prosperous life in southern Alberta. While Emma would die suddenly at 38 of a brain hemorrhage in 1920, Lambert lived to 81.[4] Just 44 when he built the Empress, Lambert would have seen 1912 as another banner year, one which continued the growth the town had enjoyed since its incorporation in 1892.

It was Macleod now, "Fort" being dropped as a sign of gentile independence from the North West Mounted Police outpost, a sanding of its frontier rough spots. It was two years before the assassination of an Austrian archduke would touch off the Great War and send Macleod's sons, of which 73 would not return, to Europe in defence of the Motherland. Sir Robert Borden, whose image now graces Canada's $100 bill, was prime minister, having just taken the reins from Sir Wilfred Laurier, who graces the $5. Some three months following Lambert's January musings, the *Advertiser* would publish news of the greatest maritime disaster of its day: the sinking of RMS *Titanic* and the loss of more than 1,500 lives in the North Atlantic, a tragedy marked by services in Macleod churches.

While the news of a "fine new opera house" was exciting and would have been welcomed in the town, it's a wonder it hadn't been built sooner. After all, by 1912 Macleod was a fully fledged community, home, according to the 1910 census, to 2,500 citizens, just 600 fewer than the 2011 head count. The town had for years enjoyed a lively cultural life, one that could only thrive with a new theatre. But then, when the economic vagaries of the time are factored, it's fortunate Thomas Martin, a well-known Macleod lawyer, pressed ahead with the Empress when he did, because when growth slowed during the war years it was unable to regain its pace when peace was restored. By then, anticipated growth and projected prosperity had slowed considerably.

So it seems the moment was right for Martin to make his move, to launch the town's first opera house. His idea came to be and, shortly afterward, the community embraced the theatre as its cultural centre. Considering the history of the place, the town's readiness was not surprising. Fort Macleod was seeded in 1874 with the arrival of the North West Mounted Police, led by Colonel James F. Macleod. During those early years as the town rivaled Lethbridge as a centre of importance in southern Alberta, Macleod gradually grew beyond the walls of the fort, both literally and figuratively. Three decades later, it was a

> SPECULATION PLACED THE COMMUNITY AT THE HUB OF MULTIPLE RAIL LINES, DRIVING UP REAL ESTATE PRICES, POPULATION AND EVERYONE'S HOPES OF A PROSPEROUS FUTURE. MACLEOD WAS GOING TO BE THE "WINNIPEG OF THE WEST."

thriving prairie community, its citizens enjoying a full scope of social activities from sports to theatre productions.

When it was originally founded on an island in the Oldman River about a mile east of the town that would bear its name, the fort was the first permanent police outpost in the British northwest. By the time the settlement had relocated a decade later to the river's south bank and west of the fort site, Macleod was gentrifying into a centre of community and commerce.

The hardships of settling and policing the Canadian prairies were monumental, work that required a hardy body and spirit. The majority of men drawn to the adventure of membership in NWMP fortunately came with a healthy amount of both. Along with the frontier mentality they possessed to see them through, they also relied on their own brand of entertainment to enjoy the few hours of respite afforded them in this grueling new world. While later artistry was reviewed by several newspapers that served the growing community, these early "performances" depended on writers such as Richard Nevitt, a member of the NWMP who arrived in 1874 at age 24.

The young American, a refugee of the U.S. Civil War, trained as a physician at Trinity College in Toronto and gained military experience as a member of the Queen's Own Rifles. Joining the NWMP allowed him to earn money to further his medical training and he headed west with the force as its surgeon. While his medical skills were no doubt appreciated in those early years, it was his ability to chronicle the life of the fort that better serves history. *A Winter at Fort Macleod*, a compilation of Nevitt's letters to his sweetheart Elizabeth Beaty, whom he later married, may well include the earliest "review" of fort entertainment, describing the evening of January 13, 1875:

> Last evening we had a number of the musical men of the Force in our Mess Room and they practiced some hymns and chants for our Sunday Service. After going over several hymns they sang some profane songs, some of which were very good indeed. Then after they had gone we enlisted one of the violinists and

> had a dance which kept us for a time well amused; then I went to bed about eleven.[5]

Sports, cricket seemingly chief among them, entertained the troops, and music and singing were always available to relieve the monotony. Nevitt detailed several incidents of sports rivalry and performances more cultural in nature. Often, groups camped in the area were invited to join the police for evenings of music and dance. On June 8, 1875, Nevitt describes such an event including the residents of a Metis encampment near the fort:

> Last night the men of "F" Troop gave a dance to the half-breeds; everyone seemed to enjoy themselves most heartily, dancing their reels and jigs. An old fiddler perched upon an elevated seat beat time with both feet and jerked head and arms about in a most remarkable manner. They kept the fun going until about midnight and Fort Macleod returned to its wonted state of repose.[6]

With incorporation 18 years later, Macleod quickly appeared to be on its way to becoming a major player in the development of the western prairies. Starting as a service centre for the area's ranching industry, the town strutted into 1911, poised to claim its place as a key railroad centre. Speculation placed the community at the hub of multiple rail lines, driving up real estate prices, population and everyone's hopes of a prosperous future. Macleod was going to be the "Winnipeg of the West."

Macleod's growth, since 1885, had been steady, first as a young town of the Northwest Territories, then, as of 1905, as a burgeoning centre in the newborn province of Alberta. The town promoted itself far and wide as the place to stake futures and make fortunes. Immigrants, mostly from the British Isles, bought out new subdivisions. Chinese, French, Italian and Dutch provided ethnic diversity as all settled in to await the coming boom.

With expansion, however, came financial growing pains in those first few years of the new century. Utilities were required (electricity arrived in 1904; the waterworks was expanded and a sewer system installed in 1908); a town office, school and other facilities common to spirited growth began to ring up debts beyond the town's ability to pay. Plans for a fancy new town hall, to replace the original which burned in 1908, were shelved due to cost.

Fire, in fact, shaped Macleod's future for the next century, and likely played a role in the ultimate shape of the Empress. In 1906, fire razed most of the wood-frame buildings on Main Street, resulting in passage of a bylaw requiring all new buildings to be constructed of brick or stone. That bylaw literally cast in stone the present-day thoroughfare, now a source of community pride. It is best described by the Town of Fort Macleod:

> Most of the two-storey brick and sandstone buildings lining the two main business thoroughfares were constructed during the pre-1914 boom years. Much of the material used was produced by local brickyards, lumber mills, and stone quarries. The masons and builders who erected the fine structures bestowed upon the town the legacy of building styles, traditional values, and craftsmanship brought with them from England. Residences of the 1897-1914 period show the same quality and attention to detail found in the downtown buildings, reflecting the availability of materials and craftsmen and an interest in predominant period styles.[7]

Unfortunately, that heady turn-of-the-century optimism began to fizzle shortly after the Empress opened. That year, the Canadian Pacific Railway, which had previously designated Macleod as a key point in its western operations, cozied up to Lethbridge instead and moved 200 jobs there. The outbreak of the First World War slowed construction; not long after the armistice, Fort Macleod had been supplanted by Lethbridge as key town in the south.[8]

If fire forged the historical wonder of Main Street by ensuring its permanence in brick and stone, its uniqueness was guaranteed by economics. Prior to 1914, hubris and optimism resulted in construction of 34 of the buildings which now comprise Fort Macleod's Provincial Historic Area.

Following the first rush to build, Macleod continued to race ahead acquiring infrastructure in anticipation of expected growth and, in doing so, burdened itself with debt. As a result, the town declared bankruptcy in 1924. The debt was paid off through a low-interest loan which, in turn, made it impossible for the town to borrow money, a circumstance that constricted growth until 1960. Ironically, this financial straightjacket is one of the reasons for the beautifully preserved buildings on today's Main Street; forced to make do with structures that arose in the early years of the 20th century, Macleod maintained what it had.

Rise M. Massey elaborates in a paper prepared for Alberta Culture:

> The optimism and expectation which prevailed produced an unprecedented building boom. Not only was there a great increase in residential building, but the majority of the brick and sandstone front commercial blocks on Twenty-fourth Street and Second Avenue were constructed; they displayed architectural characteristics seldom found in small towns.[9]

Arriving hard on the heels of the moratorium on spending, the Great Depression of the 1930s and the ensuing Second World War assured that the unique town centre with its architectural gems would remain through the century and into the new millennium.

The Empress Theatre, then, is a symbol of the town's unbound spirit throughout its formative years, a saucy little dancehall number dolled up for fun in a time of unlimited possibilities, then preserved like Pompeii under a rain of economic ash. Unlike the buildings in that unfortunate Roman town, however, the Empress lives on, both as a reminder of the past and as a beacon in its future.

One might wonder at the term "opera house" when, in fact, the Empress's chief purpose had little to do with classic opera. The naming is explained by D. Layne Elhers in *This Week at the Opera House*:

> Frontier communities regarded opera houses as visual symbols of prosperity, beacons to settlers that a town had permanence, promise and culture. Opera house suggested refinement and elegance. Frequent dances provided income for fire departments, dance schools,

lodges, bands, commercial clubs and ball teams. Home talent performances...always earned high praise from local newspaper editors.[10]

Time has erased, to a varying degree, what is known of the three men key to the inception and construction of the Empress: owner Thomas B. Martin, builder James S. Lambert and architect William T. Williams, who was then most prominent in Medicine Hat, Alberta. However, Lambert was a fixture in Macleod at the time, having been chosen to build the town's new hospital opened that year. The newspapers of the time make it clear, as far as business went, he left nothing to chance, advertising frequently.[11]

He was, no doubt, one of the businessmen who cheered the news that year that cheaper power was heading Fort Macleod's direction. The Canadian Western Natural Gas Light Heat and Power Company announced it would sell natural gas to the town to run its power house at half the price it had been paying. The Advertiser declared the new rate would allow Macleod to provide the cheapest power in Canada, with the exception of Medicine Hat, and cheered the outcome of negotiations with Great Western:

> The Town Council and Board of Trade have ever before them the prime necessity of providing some sort of cheap power as an inducement to industries to locate here. Without power, Macleod will, of necessity, remain an agricultural community for a long while to come.[12]

Lambert might also have bid on construction of the Connaught Hotel, the plans for which were front-page news in February. While it never materialized, the 85-guest hotel was planned for the south side of 21st Street at the corner of Fifth Avenue. Canada was to be punctuated with Connaught hotels, schools and other public edifices in the coming years following

the appointment, in 1911, of the Duke of Connaught as the nation's 10th governor general. Named to the post by his nephew, King George V, the duke served in the vice-regal appointment for five years.

He might have been among those who sought the contract for the new post office promised by Ottawa, one of many desired by communities across the country, a $50,000 project for which the town would supply the land. Yes, Macleod was booming and real estate was touted as a solid investment. He may have been enticed by an ad in the Advertiser that February urging all contractors to be part of the excitement forecast that spring.[13] Maybe, while reading his copy of the Advertiser, checking his own ad and ignoring come-ons for powders and potions promising remedies for all manner of medical misfortune and hair loss, Lambert briefly considered dropping into Barnes and McNay on Second Avenue for a demonstration of Thomas Alva Edison's new phonograph. The iPod of its day, it featured double the content on each record and the ability to record at home. Perhaps he considered treating himself to one of these new machines as a fitting reward for landing the Empress project. Maybe, though, he considered such a device a waste of time and money when there was a town to unpack and erect.

Area contractors would certainly have had more than a passing interest in the announcement the Crow's Nest Pass Lumber Company of British Columbia planned to develop a massive yard in Macleod to feed the prairie trade. The town's access to the CPR and, soon, the CNR, made it a choice distribution point. Again, the Advertiser was zealous in its endorsement of the project:

> ...Macleod will then possess two of the finest Transcontinental Railway connections possible to obtain and considering the natural resources of the surrounding country and the geographical location of

THE OUTBREAK OF THE FIRST WORLD WAR SLOWED CONSTRUCTION; NOT LONG AFTER THE ARMISTICE, FORT MACLEOD HAD BEEN SUPPLANTED BY LETHBRIDGE AS KEY TOWN IN THE SOUTH.

the town, Macleod is bound to become a wholesale and distributing centre of importance.[14]

Lambert could well have speculated on the success of the new Riverside Park subdivision where lots were selling for $60, $5 down and $5 a month. A speculator in 1912 could buy a building lot and a new suit at J. W. Moreash, all for a $100 bill and receive $22 change, enough to take the family to the Saturday matinee at the Lyric Theatre. If there were no need to entertain children, an outing might include something more academic in nature, such as a lecture at the Methodist Church by Professor Lewis of the University of Alberta on the theory of evolution, complete with lantern slides of amoebas.[15]

Lambert might have seen February as an opportune time to treat his wife Emma to a Valentine's Day dinner out. Where better to dine than the City Cafe, which boasted its recent hiring of "TWO OF THE BEST WHITE CHEFS IN THE WEST."[16] An alternative would have been Chow Sam Restaurant which, while it didn't brag about the colour or ethnicity of its cooks, did direct customers' attention to its "Good Meals Well Cooked and Plenty of Them." Meanwhile, a craving for oysters could be sated at the Silver Grill in the Leather Block, across the street from where the Empress would rise that year – a fine, new opera house!

Ad from 1912 issues of The Macleod Advertiser—February 8, 1912 page 5.

CHAPTER THREE
# NEW THEATRE CREDIT TO TOWN

*IN THE TIME it took Lambert to stride back to his office, William T. Williams took a final look at his plans for Macleod's new theatre and prepared to show them to Tom Martin later that day. The story in the* Advertiser *added enough flourishes of its own to make the writer a turn-of-the-century alphabetical engineer, thought Williams, but never mind. The townsfolk would have the kind of palace that befitted the prosperous community. With this completed set of drawings in hand, he could pick up his T square, return to his drawing board and continue work on designs for buildings in Lethbridge and Medicine Hat.*

*All three centres were a source of work during these last three years or so. He'd designed huge, fashionable houses for the well-to-do, some turreted, done in brick with wide porches and columns. These were mansions really, popping up like daffodils after an April snowfall, enough in Medicine Hat to populate a small village. Lethbridge had been a good place for work; his blueprints gave rise to the Whitney Block three years ago, the Chinook Club addition a year later and then the Goodman Block on Third Avenue South. But now, this change of plans: an opera theatre in Macleod, and with the dust from the last great buffalo herds barely settled.*

*Williams had thrown several architectural styles into his design for Martin's theatre; his plan was an eclectic blend, an architectural jumble of bits stolen from here and there. The arch he had fashioned in the Beaux-Arts tradition was most pleasing. Common practice, creative licence, thought Williams, typical of a century so young it had yet to develop a form of its own.*

*Well, why not add a little dollop of Paree to his creation? The Empress's arch, he believed, would be its grand architectural gesture, his and the building's one chance to make a statement. He'd included other unique touches, too, though; after all, this building might wind up as the pre-eminent opera house in southern Alberta for years to come. He was also proud of his inclusion of spandrels, or, as he'd explained to Lambert, the ornate inserts used to fill in corners where rounded shapes such as arches are placed into right angled spaces, like a round peg in a square hole, and the oculus, the round window in the projection room on the second floor, to give the poor sod stuck up there in the summer's heat something to look out in between changing movie reels.*

*And he'd see to it Lambert built it right, hardy enough to stand up to the infernal cycle of heat and cold and winds strong enough to shake foundations from here to heaven. Granted, the stage seemed a trifle puny, but that wasn't his call; it was dictated by the size of Martin's lot. And the theatre would have no "flies," no room aloft for storing scenery. Still, he'd specified a tin-plated ceiling which should stand for a few years, and tin crown moulding on the sides painted to look like wood; lighter and cheaper.*

*To add depth, the top front corners were pulled up and out. The arch leading into the barrel vault and the ticket booth – domed, multi-sided, and circled in lights – would draw the attention of people on the street. And, once they gained entrance, patrons would pass through two mirrored doors.*

*For the theatre's floor, he'd decided on hardwood maple; for the walls, plaster and burlap. He'd curved the stage to project two feet beyond the proscenium at the middle. His plans called for three dressing rooms in the basement, along with a bathroom, baggage room, boiler room and fuel storage room.*

*Williams took another look at the* Advertiser's *story and finished preparing the plans to show Martin that evening. Considering the chancy weather in these parts, Martin might have wished for lobby space, but what the plans delivered was what Tom requested: a basic theatre typical of the time. So, the audience might have to huddle in the cold to buy tickets; at least there'd be more seats for which to sell tickets. No, considering all that had been incorporated into the design, Williams was pretty sure he had a winner that would rival the* Morris, *opened last year in Lethbridge, and the two planned for opening later this year, the* Majestic *and the city's own* Empress.

*The architect understood the importance of Empresses, Princesses, Monarchs and all manner of royally named buildings to the colonial lifestyle Macleod and other prairie towns were desperate to build, nurture and maintain. Regardless of what level of royalty this new theatre would eventually be named for, it would be far more than a mere opera house; it would stand as an edifice of optimism, a place the people of Macleod could call their own, a gathering spot in which to come together for cultural evenings, celebrating their own talents or relishing those of traveling troupes and actors on the screen. Sure of Martin's appreciation of the scope of the creation, Williams flipped through the blueprints one last time. Then, after aligning their margins, he carefully rolled the sheets, speculating all the while that his design might even delight the entrepreneur.*

While liberties have been taken here in delving into Williams' thoughts a century ago, his musings are underpinned with fact. Williams continued to practise in Medicine Hat for another three or four years after completing plans for the Empress before moving his business to Pasadena, California. Born in Bristol, England, Williams, at 10, immigrated to Detroit, Michigan, in 1885 with his parents and a brother, Albert. In 1900, he graduated from Boston College where he had studied architecture, married Edith Davis, a Canadian some seven years his senior, and entered into an international business of sorts with his brother Albert. As half of the Williams Brothers, William moved to Windsor, Ontario to serve Canadian clients, while Albert stayed in Detroit to manage the American side of the firm.

In 1905, while in Medicine Hat, his vision had become manifest in several prominent city buildings, including the Town Hall, a majority of the town's schools, the Stewart & Tweed Block, Porter Block and the Cypress Club. Opening an office in Lethbridge had led to considerable business in that city, too, including the Chinook Club, Westminster School, the Western Canada Agency warehouse and industrial buildings in the fairgrounds.[1]

Long before Williams began his design for the Empress theatre, he would have been well acquainted with the Beaux-Arts style of architecture. Small wonder he saw fit to incorporate it into his design for the theatre. Beaux-Arts, developed in France, really took root in Europe in the late 18th century and flourished for more than 150 years, enjoying particular favour throughout North America.[2] The form borrowed from French and Italian Baroque and Rococo styles. A wing of the Louvre in Paris is finished in Beaux Arts, while the architectural style played a role in the 1893 Chicago World's Columbian Exposition. The concept for the centre of the exposition, White City, was completed in Beaux-Arts.[3] Closer to home, Beaux-Arts architecture was the inspiration for the legislature buildings of Alberta, Saskatchewan and Manitoba and, among other notable buildings, the Hockey Hall of Fame in Toronto (originally a Bank of Montreal built in 1885) and the Supreme Court of Canada in Ottawa.[4]

With the work completed, the architect left these prairie locales which had been a canvas for his creativity, and moved his business to Pasadena, California.

*While Williams congratulated himself on his architectural flair, Thomas Martin was more than a little anxious after reading that day's* Advertiser. *There it was for the world to read, on the front page, as he knew it would be, the story of his plans for the lot on 24th, recounted in robust hyperbole demonstrating the newspaper's need to aggrandize every town development. He could build a new outhouse in the middle of the street and the* Advertiser *would describe it as a block of suites on the Champs-Elysees, a great addition to the appearance of the town's chief thoroughfare.*

*Martin hoped the theatre would be a valuable addition to the community, now that the news was in the town rags. He hoped he was doing the right thing. Why was he, a lawyer, getting himself involved in the theatre business anyway, especially considering the town already had three of them and, as the* Advertiser *described it, the wretched town hall. Maybe if he had wanted to invest in theatre, he should have returned to the east. After all, he was only 40 and he had already spent six years in Macleod; perhaps it was time for a change. But Cayuga, Ontario, was a memory. So, here he was investing in the future of the Canadian West and being declared as the saviour of the theatre, right there on the front page.*

*Well, in for a penny, in for a pound. He had bought the lot from Chow Sam, a prominent town businessman. William had designed the theatre and James would build it. Perhaps the place would afford his family something to carry them should his damnable diabetes do its worst. He wished Ed could give him some advice. But now that his old law partner was Judge Edward McNeill, the two didn't see as much of each other, not like they did when they set up practice here in 1906 in the newly created province nor in the six years following.*

*Instead, he relied on Ruby for her guidance. He knew he was lucky to have married Ruby Gwendolyn Foster, who had given him little Gwenda and Barney. At least this crazy real estate venture would provide the children a place to watch their* Mutt *and* Jeff *shows, silly though they were. Well, to home; Ruby would be waiting and he could review the plans with Lambert tomorrow. Ah, yes, Williams had created the idea, now the able Lambert would bring it to reality. James Lambert, with his rough-hewn English accent and his wonderful ability to create masterful buildings such as that McDonnell Block. The work was truly inspired. What was it James had called it? Romanesque Revival or some such exotic term? Who cared, as long as the man brought his considerable skills to bear on this theatre.*

While little has been written about Thomas Martin, he was definitely a man about town.[5] The Empress was not the first locale in town for the enjoyment of theatre beyond the police barracks. Long before the idea of an opera house entered Martin's mind, theatre had moved to other locales in town. In early 1886, townsfolk turned out for the opening of the community's first town hall, a two-storey structure intended to serve as a court of law, a school and, on the main floor, local recreation. In fact, even the mere whisper of the possibility of a town hall had sent a flutter through the theatrical community's breast. Once opened, they trod the boards of its lower level for some 26 years until the opening of the Empress.[6]

Nor was the town hall the only venue prior to the Empress. The Maple Leaf, Majestic and Lyric (opened in a former furniture store on 24th Street in 1911)[7] all predated the Empress, showing movies, or photo plays as early films were called, and boasting of their "refined entertainment." (If anything, Macleod might have been over-theatred; the Empress alone, with 500 original seats, provided one of every five of the town's 2,500 citizens with a seat.) Of the three, the Lyric, also on Twenty-fourth Street, was perhaps best able to compete with the newcomer, but four months after the Empress opened, the Lyric went up in flames.[8] According to news reports of the day, the "charred ruin" left behind by the fire had been earlier considered due for demolition regardless. Thus, the fire seemed little more than a fast track to urban renewal and the Empress was left to reign alone. Fire safety, however, was at the time a key point in new construction, especially in movie houses which incorporated highly flammable film. The Empress, then, would have been constructed to the town's fire regulation bylaw enacted in 1902 and strengthened in 1912.[9]

> EMPRESS HAD BEEN WATCHED, TALKED ABOUT AND WRITTEN UP IN THE LOCAL PRESS SO OFTEN, ITS CONSTRUCTION COULD HAVE BEEN LIKENED TO THE BIRTHING OF A ROYAL PRINCESS.

Prior to assuming its place on the town's theatrical throne, the Empress had been watched, talked about and written up in the local press so often, its construction could have been likened to the birthing of a royal princess. "The queen is dead, long live the queen" quickly became the sentiment expressed, at least in print, of the ascendency of the Empress as a seat of culture over the old town hall. Of course, the "old town hall" was itself a monumental improvement from the NWMP barracks. Time marched on and, as the idea of a new theatre took hold, loyalties shifted and the town hall fell out of favour; newspapers were unkind, describing the place as "wretched." With the arrival of the Empress looming, the press, caught in a bit of a media stampede, rushed in to report the details.

Theatre Watch, 1912 edition:

Feb. 1, 1912: "The piano for the new theatre has arrived, so they are all ready for the music, at all events."[10]

March 14: "Contractor Lambert has the long timber out for the new theatre, but it is too cold to start the concrete work yet."[11]

Early May: "The brickfront of the new theatre makes an imposing showing on 24th street."[12]

June 4: "The handsome moving picture theatre which is being created on Twenty-fourth street by T. B. Martin will be completed in about two weeks, and it is expected that it will be opened to the public on July 1."[13]

June 6: "The new theatre may be opened on the 15th [of June], Contractor Lambert thinks. It is to be named the 'Dreamland'..."[14]

June 13: "The plastering is nearly dry in the new Dreamland Theatre and the floor is down."[15]

At this point, the name of the theatre had not actually been confirmed; that was the call of lessees Lotz and McRae, Medicine Hat theatre operators, who planned to use it as a moving-picture house. R. J. McRae operated the Dreamland in Medicine Hat and the Empress in Vernon, B.C., so at this point, the choice of names balanced on a geographical knife edge. As it turned out, the decision was postponed as the new baby wasn't born on June 15, its expected date of arrival. The probable cause of the delay: rampant construction in Macleod during June. The *Advertiser* was there to record the sights and sounds of building: "The sound of the hammer and saw are heard in Macleod from seven o'clock in the morning until six o'clock in the evening."[16] All this hammering and sawing was not in aid of throwing up cheap wooden buildings. Many of the projects being completed in this time were to become the pride of the town, then as today lasting monuments to the community's promise and potential.

Finally, slightly more than five months after it was announced in the *Advertiser*, the theatre opened on Saturday, June 29 and, to no great surprise, it was named the Empress. Press reports are meager concerning the interior of the building. All the *Advertiser* could manage was a mention of "up-to-date chairs and appliances," calling it a "beautiful place of amusement." There is no mention of the entertainment presented that day, or, indeed, if the opening was anything more than a public tour of the facility.[17] Two weeks later, the *Spectator* noted a "handsome new electric sign" was being installed that day.

It seems a little odd that after months of news items detailing each step of construction, from the arrival of the piano back in February to the description of the drying plaster in mid-June, media reports were rather subdued when the Empress finally opened. Marselle Jobs Thompson, in her richly researched 1990 master's thesis on the Empress, wonders if perhaps the town's press boys were not invited to the event.[18] A possibility also exists there was a falling out between the newspapers and the Empress management, perhaps over access, perhaps over advertising. Regardless, it took until mid-August, almost two months after the opening, for a full story on the town's new showplace to finally appear in print. By its headline, the *Spectator* appears to have gotten the scoop: "New Theatre Credit to Town: Spectator Man Shown Through Empress by Manager McRae, Who Has String of Similar Houses."[19]

In the news story, the Spectator suggests a disconnect between theatre management and the community's amateur theatre groups who had been clamouring for a proper facility in which to present their performances. The article mentions McRae's intention to use the Empress for movies and professional touring theatre, but fails to indicate if local productions will be welcome. Perhaps McRae, from Medicine Hat, supposed the amateur players of Macleod would fail to live up to the prestige he wanted to project for his new venue.

It was true, the Empress was open and operating, if a trifle less grandly than anticipated in press reports earlier that year. By winter, that difference and the resulting friction it caused between owner and manager, was obvious.

*DECEMBER already and damn this place. And damn the people of Macleod who don't seem to understand he, R. J. McRae, was not operating the Empress as a charity. No, he was an entrepreneur, in the theatre business – if he could still call it a business – to make money. He required the Empress to make an acceptable return on his investment. He wasn't here to cater to local talent shows and provincial stage plays. He'd tried giving what they wanted, and, to be sure, the Paul Gilmore company had filled the place in October, but a full house was rare and Gilmore was costly to bring in. And now this debacle.*

*As he'd explained to that writer from the* Advertiser *last month, he enjoyed presenting good professional entertainment but, after all, he also had to make a dollar. Didn't these people get it? He had to guarantee these companies left town with a specified amount or they wouldn't come this far off the main circuit. Once the company in November was paid off, he wound up with $2.75 in profit. Two dollars and six bits. He'd be damned sure Martin wouldn't lease his theatre for a $2.75 profit each night. And the worst of it was after he'd paid for promotions, staff and other expenses, he was $40 in the hole. He'd even lost money on the Gilmore deal. If this kept up, he'd be bankrupt by Easter. As he'd told the reporter, if folks in Macleod wanted good theatre, they were going to have to start patronizing it or they could be satisfied with picture shows from here to high water. He'd thought his quote to the scribbler was pretty decent and direct: he couldn't live off the winds here and the good wishes of the townsfolk.*

*Now, a break-in. He couldn't get people to come through the front door, but they were all too happy to come through the rear and steal more than six dollars from his till. He hoped they choked on it, all in nickels and dimes. He was being nickeled and dimed into debt. Maybe it was an inside job; the police suspected as much since all the doors were locked Monday morning. Pried the lock off the drawer in the box office, the thieves did, and could have made off with considerably more had they known how much he kept in his office desk drawer. That would have made for a merry New Year's Eve for the scoundrels. Maybe he should pack it in here and move to Vernon, enjoy the sunshine, the lakes and the mild winters. Damn.*

CHAPTER FOUR

# MACLEOD EVIDENTLY DOESN'T CARE FOR VAUDEVILLE

Poor R. J.; still, he soldiered on[1] and, in the true spirit of entrepreneurship, found ways to bring in more money. He made it through the Empress' first winter of 1912-13, presumably with no more break-ins or theft and, in May 1913, announced intentions to install a drop curtain on which businesses could place advertisements for the edification of crowds waiting for performances to start. Presumably, some firms did take out ads on the curtain, perhaps as a sign of their business acumen, perhaps because they wanted to support the theatre.

In October, McRae decided to upgrade the theatre, deepening the stage by ten feet and improving sightlines and seating. C. W. Stephens was hired to do the renovations in the evenings. Again, the press performed as cheerleaders, with the *Spectator* suggesting the improvements would afford Macleod a "Real Theatre with a Good Stage, Inclined Floor, and Opera Chairs." Each seat would "give the occupant a chance to see without taking all the rubber out of his neck."[2] It's possible, as Jobs Thompson notes in her dissertation, McRae had either improved his financial situation to where he could afford these alterations, or believed they were necessary to book larger, better-known acts to attract bigger gates. Closely following *The Beggar Prince* was *The Last Waltz*, a performance by Pollard's Australian Juvenile Opera Co.

In *The Pollards*, writer Peter Downes explains how this amazing troupe, comprised of child performers, was formed in Tasmania in 1880. For three decades, Pollard opera companies toured Australia, New Zealand and North America, performing the latest operettas of the day, including works by William Gilbert and Arthur Sullivan:

> The youngsters reached the top of their profession, but only after exhausting work, harsh opposition and much anguish. Brushes with cholera and smallpox mix with accustations [sic] of kidnapping and suicide; disastrous fires destroy scenery, costumes and music; bankruptcy looms; tumultuous storms at sea threaten to shorten their lives. Yet, through it all, the Pollards emerge unscathed, to act and sing joyously for their adoring public. Throughout the western world the allure of child actors in adult roles seemed endless, but social disapproval eventually brought about their demise. But of the many teams of talented youngsters traversing the world at the end of the 19th century,

the Pollard companies appear to have been the most enterprising and enduring of them all.[3]

The Pollard troupe wasn't the only one featuring children in adult roles. In *Juvenile Opera Companies*, Stephen Busch explains Gilbert & Sullivan mania had swept the globe, and most juvenile companies performed their works, in particular *HMS Pinafore*. Many arose in the United States with names such as Boston Miniature Ideal Opera Company, and many performances were pirated under loose copyright laws. Busch quotes an 1882 *New York Times* article detailing concerns about the use of children in these companies:

> President Eldridge T. Gerry of the Society for the Prevention of Cruelty to Children made a long and earnest plea to Mayor Grace not to give the desired permission. It was a shame, he argued, to compel young children to perform night after night and rehearse day after day in such broiling weather merely to put money into the pockets of the managers.
>
> Mr. Gerry spoke at length of the bad moral influences surrounding such juvenile troupes, and instanced many cases where his society had been asked to try to reclaim young girls from lives of vice into which they had been led while employed on the stage. A list of names was submitted to the Mayor from which it appeared that of the 65 members of the company, about 20 were under 16, and hence required the Mayor's consent before they could perform. Mayor Grace glanced over the list and drew his pen through the names of three whose ages were 11 years or under.[4]

These were, then, fairly major acts McRae was presenting at the Empress. The aforementioned Paul Gilmore (1873–1962) was a popular American stage actor of 10 silent films who operated his own touring companies and cast himself in roles as a swashbuckling lover in plays such as *Captain Debonnaire*, *The Mummy* and the *Hummingbird* and *The Boys of Company B*.[5]

So, were the townsfolk not filling the seats in reasonable numbers when these international acts graced the Empress stage, or was McRae merely hoping to make more money by moaning to the media? It's hard to determine, but at least McRae kept the acts coming. And they were diverse: movies were interspersed with a political rally, local drama performances and more traveling troupes throughout 1913-14. Did Macleod movie fans have a chance to see *Traffic in Souls*, one of the year's best? If so, local sensibilities might have been ruffled: the movie detailed sex-slave trafficking, starring Mary Barton and Matt Moore, and was banned in several locations. Other hits of 1913 included *Matrimony's Speed Limit*, *David Copperfield*, *Hamlet*, *The Prisoner of Zenda*, *The Gangsters*, *The Mothering Heart*, *The Pickwick Papers* and one from Quebec-born Mac Sennett, *A Noise from the Deep*. Sennett would make a career producing slapstick comedies featuring stars such as Charlie Chaplin, The Keystone Kops and W.C. Fields.

Between the movies, McRae even offered wrestling matches.[6] Perhaps grappling fans were able, prior to his retirement that April, to cheer for wrestling legend Frank Gotch, an American who ruled the sport throughout North America and claimed the title "Champion of the Klondike." Or maybe they cheered for Ed "Strangler" Lewis, rated as the most skilled and dangerous wrestler in the game, that year's world champion.

McRae, it seems, took a brief break from daily duties at the Empress and handed control to Manager Scougall.[7] He was back in charge by mid-July 1914. A month later, McRae was again bemoaning his finances in the press, suggesting townsfolk were staying home rather than attend the vaudeville performances he was taking pains to offer them at the Empress. He certainly had the *Spectator* in his corner, which chided readers' recalcitrance in August:

> Macleod evidently doesn't care for vaudeville. Manager McRae of the Empress had a number of Pantages acts here last night and they were all good acts too, but the people did not turn out in very large numbers. The result was a considerable financial loss to Mr. McRae.

Photo Courtesy: Robert Hart

*Blackface* – Local minstrel group at the Empress Theatre circa 1920. Photo courtesy Bob Hart whose father Henry (Ding) Hart and uncle Alfred Hart appear second and third from left respectively.

The acts were all faultless. There was an animal act, which was clever, while the musical turn was excellent. The Spectator hopes that Mr. McRae will not be discouraged with one tidal but will bring these fine Pantages performers here again. Perhaps next time there will be a larger audience.[8]

The journalistic support afforded the impresario exceeds what might be expected by presenters today; most performances seemed to rate rave reviews and townspeople who chose not to buy tickets were excoriated for their decision.

By this time, the Empress had been used to stage hospital aid benefits, lectures, operas, political rallies (R. B. Bennett held a political rally on April 10, 1913, several years before becoming prime minister), concerts, plays, animated pictures, and minstrel shows, all in its first two years. Companies included the Delhi Durbars, the Hallowell Concert Company, Beggar Prince Opera and Richard's and Pringle's (Famous Georgia) Minstrels.

The minstrel show, or minstrelsy, was an American entertainment consisting of comic skits, variety acts, dancing, and music, performed by white people in blackface or, especially after the Civil War, black people in blackface. One has to remember the era in which minstrel shows were drawing crowds to the Empress; it's hardly likely they would be tolerated today. Minstrel shows portrayed black people as ignorant, lazy, buffoonish, superstitious, joyous and musical. The minstrel show began in the early 1830s and emerged as a full-fledged form in the next decade. In its heyday, the typical minstrel performance followed a three-act structure. The troupe first danced onto stage to exchange wisecracks and sing songs. The second part featured a variety of entertainments, including the pun-filled stump speech, while a final act consisted of a slapstick musical plantation skit or a send-up of a popular play.

They were finally overshadowed by vaudeville, but survived as professional entertainment until about 1910. In the United States, however, amateur performances continued until the 1960s in high schools, fraternities and local theaters. As African Americans began to score legal and social victories against racism and to successfully assert political power, minstrelsy lost popularity.[9]

By late 1914, after a year of films such as *The Body in the Trunk, The Face on the Bar Room Floor* and *The Girl in the Shack*, several Chaplin flicks and fare with such prurient titles as *Twenty Minutes of Love, Old Enough to Be Her Grandpa* and *Damaged Goods*, the local theatergoer was treated to the first of many entertaining evenings by the Empress house orchestra, which provided background music for silent movies and added to other performances. The trio featured: on violin, C. R. Newton; on piano, Mrs. Kerr Seymour; and on trombone, H. L. Field. True to form, the *Spectator* offered effusive praise: "Macleod should certainly be grateful and appreciate the management for the way the comforts of the patrons are considered."[10]

Of the three members of the orchestra, violinist Newton appears to have struck a resonance with the *Spectator's* reviewer, who praised his bowing skills and his singing ability and predicted a promising musical career for the young man:

> ...the bright, particular star of the evening was Mr. Newton, whose violin selections gave the greatest pleasure to his auditors. Mr. Newton's technique is little short of marvelous, and it is quite apparent that he is a highly trained musician. His selections were all encored enthusiastically, and he was generous in responding.[11]

So, Macleod's Empress was a centre of entertainment in the community, offering fare ranging from elegant violin virtuosos to sweaty wrestlers.

In August 1915, just as he had three years earlier, McRae faced a financial threat, this time from Thomas Martin's lease demands. The result was the first major upset for the three-year-old Empress, which was about to lose its first tenant to Macleod's "wretched" town hall, all the result of a landlord-tenant dispute worthy of a match between Frank Gotch and "Strangler" Lewis. Their tiff could be described as a bit of a wrestling match.

*Round One:* "Terrible" Thomas Martin takes R. J. "Mauler" McRae to the mat with what fight fans later declare are overcharged rents for use of the Empress. McRae attempts to get out from under Martin's lease, but fails to dislodge his fearsome opponent.

*Round Two:* After much exertion, "Mauler" manages to throw over Martin in a desperate effort to regain his financial standing. In his first offensive move of the match, McRae closes his operation at the Empress and convinces town council to lease him the town hall. This request is granted, and McRae quickly becomes the crowd favourite. Cheers resound throughout the arena, and the Mauler's operation in the hall quickly becomes known as the People's Theatre.

As described by those at ringside:

> Assisted by loyal staff, Mr. McRae at once proceeded to fix up the Hall and by arduous work had his plant installed last evening. The show, as usual, was excellent, and a parody on "Are We Downhearted," sung by Mr. Newton simply brought down the house... For the past three years Mr. McRae has been connected with the Empress Theatre, and has undoubtedly given his patrons satisfaction during that time, and practically every resident of the town will wish him success in his new venture.[12]

*Round Three:* Stunned by Mauler's inventive ring move, Terrible Tom, his theatre now shuttered, clears his head and proceeds to reopen the Empress, offering movies and the Empress orchestra, which apparently remained with the building. He runs in direct opposition to his old tenant as the two giants of Macleod entertainment continue their battle.[13]

*Round Four:* The match tumbles into a November town council meeting, with council jumping over the ropes and proceeding to goad McRae and his People's Theatre with higher rents of its own. There was a buck to be made in this dust-up, and council seems determined to make as many as it can. McRae seeks a

longer lease. Martin argues that council should cease leasing the facility to McRae at any price, thereby ending competition with the Empress. Martin argues that if council is to rent McRae the hall, it should be raised substantially. Council splits, with some members favouring a $50 lease, others holding out for $100, and one opposing any lease (probably wasn't a movie fan). Finally, council ends the round by following the sage advice of Councillor John L. Fawcett who suggests the town should not forgo the opportunity to make money from the lease just to protect the interests of Martin and the Empress. McRae leaves with his lease, but the rent is pegged at $100.[14]

*Round Five:* As the fight continues, two things are apparent: one, McRae is easily the fan favourite and continues to draw audiences in the town hall. Judging by the support in the press, they'd likely show up if he set up a projector against the side of the American Hotel. Two, Martin's Empress is by far the more congenial place in which to watch a film. Besides, McRae is showing only picture shows, not the lavish stage productions he was able to present at the Empress, and there's no indication Martin is filling that void. Finally, cooler heads prevail and an undisclosed deal is reached between the two grapplers. McRae returns to the Empress and Martin again has a steady income from the rent. Once again, the *Spectator* was cheering from the sidelines:

> A decided surprise was sprung on the capacity house at the People's theatre last Friday night when Mr. McRae put an announcement on the screen to the effect that the theatre would be closed after the shows on the following night. This was followed immediately by a second announcement saying that he would re-open the Empress on Monday night. The first announcement brought a surprised gasp from everybody, while the

> MACLEOD'S EMPRESS WAS A CENTRE OF ENTERTAINMENT IN THE COMMUNITY, OFFERING FARE RANGING FROM ELEGANT VIOLIN VIRTUOSOS TO SWEATY WRESTLERS.

second, to put it mildly, brought down the house. The people of Macleod have surprised even themselves by their continued loyalty to Mr. McRae, a man who knows his business, and we join with them in wishing him every success back at his old stand.[15]

The outcome was likely fortuitous for both men and the community, because with McRae ensconced at the Empress, large crowds began showing up for movies and touring productions. The *Spectator* cleared up the matter of financial returns, explaining that if those attending the "theatre on Tuesday evening last had the impression that Macleod was broke, they would have gone away with quite a different idea."[16]

Bonus: the turnouts ended McRae's public appeals for larger crowds. Perhaps the townsfolk realized how close they had come to losing access to the films of the day by not patronizing McRae earlier. Or, perhaps the movies were getting better: 1916 offered *Intolerance*, D.W. Griffith's apology for his racially intolerant *Birth of a Nation* a year earlier, a slew of Chaplin films including *The Curse of Quon Gwon*, *Snow White*, *Joan of Arc* and *Lass of the Lumberlands*.

The quiet prosperity that settled in at the Empress following the Martin-McRae title fight was ended in 1916 by a new tax grab by the Alberta government; the legislature wanted in on the entertainment action. In May, theatre fans learned of the tax in the *Spectator*, again with an opinion from R. J. McRae. The theatre tax took a penny from every movie ticket; 2½ cents on a ticket for a road show costing less than $1; and a nickel on tickets worth $1 and up. Patrons, as well as purchasing their performance ticket, were required to purchase a separate tax ticket and place it in an assigned box, which was then collected by an agent of the government. Fans had the option of buying blocks of five tax tickets, which could be used anywhere in Alberta.

The *Spectator*, generous with words, yet stingy on punctuation, explained McRae's concern:

Manager McRae looks for a certain amount of confusion and inconvenience and expects to be talked

hoarse with explanations until the good people become accustomed to this new tax, but as he, along with all other theatre managers, has to abide by the law and is under heavy bond to see that this law is carried out he hopes that the people will take this new tax with as good a grace as possible and do as much as in their power to help him avoid confusion and delays at the ticket office.[17]

Finally, for reasons unknown to the *Spectator* or any other town newspaper, McRae decided to leave the theatre frontier and head back to the civilized East a month after the implementation of the government's tax.[18]

INTO THE VOID that June of 1916 stepped C. F. Bowker, the Empress' new manager, who, in a letter to the *Spectator's* readers, promised to retain and continue the high standard of entertainment set by his predecessor. He vowed to secure a new violinist, as the Empress seems to have been without an orchestra for some time, and asked for the town's support:

> In conclusion I would say that I am here to provide you with the class of entertainment you want and in order that I may be able to give you this, your co-operation and support are necessary and which I feel confident will be forthcoming.[1]

Once again, the *Spectator* was quick with praise. Less than two months after Bowker took over theatre operations, it ran a story commenting on the "first-class films,"[2] and, three weeks later, was agog over the theatre's new three-piece orchestra.

By early September, the hunt for a violinist ended with the hiring of a Professor J. A. Little, who arrived from Calgary to take his place in the Empress orchestra and teach violin in Macleod. The *Macleod News* had the story:

> J. A. Little is open to accept pupils for the violin and piano. Mr. Little studied violin with one of [Charles-Auguste] De Beriot's favourite pupils. De Beriot was founder of the famous Franco-Belgian School of Music... and the piano theory and harmony under Dr. Bleukiron of the London College of Music.[3]

With the music situation shored, Bowker was free to search for the entertainment his patrons had come to enjoy under the departed McRae. He was soon earning raves in the press: "Manager Bowker should be congratulated on the play at the Empress theatre last Monday night," read a review in the December 7 edition of the *Macleod News*.[4] The play was *Peg 'O My Heart*, a comedy written in 1912 by J. Hartley Manners and turned into a film of the same name in 1933. That smash was followed a week later by the First World War documentary by Charles Urban, *Britain Prepared*, made at the invitation of the War Propaganda Bureau.[5] Although the naval sequences in the film were filmed in Kinemacolor, the first natural-colour process for motion pictures, the general release version of the film was in monochrome. When premiered a year earlier, the film ran into opposition in America because it promoted a message of preparedness, the United States being, at that time, neutral.[6] The *Macleod News* praised Bowker for his efforts in "...securing for Macleod audiences a program of this description."[7] Bowker also, in 1916, installed exhaust fans to circulate air every 10 minutes, aiding in patrons' comfort in the midst of hot summers.

Although the *Macleod News* had suggested a month earlier that *Peg 'O My Heart* would be difficult to beat, it predicted in January 1917 that *In Walked Jimmy* might just become the new stage champion.[8] *In Walked Jimmy*, an *American Comedy of Optimism in Four Acts*, written by Minnie Zuckerberg Jaffa in 1896, was heralded as the play of the season for its January 9 presentation at the Empress. It starred George Summers and what the

CHAPTER FIVE

# FORGET ALL ABOUT THE 'FLU. COME TO THE EMPRESS TO BE AMUSED

*News* described as a "corking cast of fifteen New York actors."[9] Tickets, available at Ferguson's Drug Store, normally ran $1 for a reserved seat, 50 to 75 cents for general admission, and two-bits for a child's seat. While the image of a cast of New York actors may have tempted the manager to push up prices for *In Walked Jimmy*, Bowker decided not to. The *News* relayed to readers its hope that a full house would turn out for this "Metropolitan production."

It was 1917, a year of Charlie Chaplin (*The Cure, Easy Street, The Adventurer, The Immigrant*) and westerns from directors such as William S. Hart (*The Gun Fighters, The Narrow Trail*) and John Ford (*Straight Shooting*). Foreign films, too, began popping up, including efforts from Sweden, Russia, Argentina and Japan.

Ending the year on a high note, the Empress announced a new house orchestra contracted to play every night and at Saturday matinees. Snatched by Bowker from their posts at the Palliser Hotel in Calgary, came Britons Fred C. Cutler and Clarice May. The duet made its first appearance November 5 initiating a standard presentation of musical accompaniment for movies and for local concerts as well as offering a special musical program at no extra charge, prompting the *Macleod News* to trumpet "this will undoubtedly be the greatest money's worth ever offered to the public."[10] Music certainly pumped up the action in silent films and, as a bonus, drowned out the sound of the projector. As Jobs Thompson concludes in her dissertation, "musical accompaniment offered by the Empress was clearly important to the patrons of the theatre at that time."[11]

Playing accompanist to silent movies was its own art form, a talent unto itself, says Dennis James, who has made a career of it since the 1970s and has played at the Empress as recently as November 2010. In the early days, movies would arrive at theatres with the sheet music included to be played, perhaps, on a piano, by a small combo or, in James's case, on an organ. James, who lives in upper New York state, is a movie historian as well as a musician and keeps faithfully to the original scores, many of which were written for specific movies by composers such as Eugene Ormandy, Richard Strauss and George Gershwin. Often, musicians who accompanied movies were among the highest paid, earning more than those in orchestras. It was, says James, a more desirable gig.

Only 17 per cent of silent movies have survived, James says, but many of the silents, as with films today, were far from Oscar material. Newspaper accounts and musicians' recollections have helped preserve their scores, much of which came from French café music, circa 1895. Of all performance arts from that era, playing for silent movies is the only one that is still practised. "It's time travel; when the movie starts, that's the way it was. It's preserving an art form. It's what the theatre was built for. People see colours, hear actors speaking; it's magical and personal."[12]

> "IT'S TIME TRAVEL; WHEN THE MOVIE STARTS, THAT'S THE WAY IT WAS. IT'S PRESERVING AN ART FORM. IT'S WHAT THE THEATRE WAS BUILT FOR. PEOPLE SEE COLOURS, HEAR ACTORS SPEAKING; IT'S MAGICAL AND PERSONAL."

At least one Fort Macleod resident can attest to James' description. Daisy Young's life has gone by in lockstep with that of the Empress. She was born in the year the Empress turned eight, and the two have intertwined experiences ever since. Young spent all but the first five years of her life in Macleod, moving there from Granum. As a 19-year-old she, too, entertained crowds at the theatre with her piano stylings played before the curtain lifted and during intermissions. She made $3 a performance, good money considering the times and her age. Though she recollects those occasions with fondness, she affirms that her memories of the Empress predate her time at the keyboard.

"Mom would drive us in to Macleod from Granum to shop and would put us in the theatre," Young recalls, leaving Young and her siblings to enjoy a movie while her mother made her rounds. Later, Young took the stage as a Grade 7 student, played in town talent shows (a professional adjudicator would be brought from Lethbridge) and, as a developing pianist, provided music for dance classes and for Florence Carstairs' annual show. "The theatre had a small orchestra pit containing a regular piano, with a railing, in the middle below the stage. I played every night when I was about 19. I remember playing before *Gone With The Wind*. The theatre really got used back then."[13]

By 1918, the Empress was back on her throne, dazzling audiences with the performances Bowker found for them. Movies remained a staple, with titles such as *A Child of the Prairie* starring Tom Mix; *The Forbidden City* with Norma Talmadge; and *A Modern Musketeer* with Douglas Fairbanks. Italian heart-throb Rudolph Valentino scorched the screen in *A Married Virgin* and *All Night*; organized crime took a hit in *Finger of Justice*; and Cecil B. DeMille laid the foundation for psychological thrillers with *The Whispering Chorus*.

The end of the year brought triumph and tragedy to Macleod and the rest of Canada: the Great War ended in victory for allied forces, allowing Canadian soldiers to begin their slow return home from four long years of bloodshed, while the world found a new way to die at the hands of the Spanish Influenza epidemic. The Empress had survived the war, bringing lightness to a dark time on the home front. Its doors were always open to offer a place of escape for the community as a whole, and particularly for those with sons and husbands in Europe's trenches. But even an Empress couldn't escape the flu; a month before the armistice on November 11, 1918, the epidemic forced mandatory closure of most public buildings in Alberta.

By early October, the flu had reached Macleod, cutting down entire families and wiping out more people worldwide than had the war. The Empress, as with all theatres, schools and places of public congregation, closed October 18 as health authorities did what they could to slow the contagion. The theatre remained shuttered until December 2, when the local board of health determined the epidemic had passed. In a misguided attempt

Photo Courtesy: Georgia Tomik

Local dance recital held at the Empress circa 1930s. Photo is courtesy Georgia (Rutledge) Tomik. Georgia appears in the second row from rear, 8th from right. Her sister Shirley Rutledge is back row, 7th from right; teacher Florence Carstairs back row, far right; and piano accompanist Daisy (Field) Young back row, 2nd from right.

to protect patrons from the flu's persistence, those enticed back into the Empress were required by management to wear masks, which had been worn in public throughout the epidemic and had done almost nothing to stop the spread of the virus:

> On October 25, it became law that everyone, when outside his home, would wear a mask of cheesecloth. These masks were worn for two hours and then thoroughly boiled before re-use. Many people wore a bag of camphor hung under their chins, which supposedly killed the germs. It has since been proven that these precautions were of no value.[14]

The *Macleod News* assured patrons they could purchase masks at the theatre should they forget to bring their own, and that the building would be fumigated and cleaned before opening:

> Bang goes the flu – the war is over... The Kaiser is defeated and the local health board declare the 'flu is also in the has-been class and that it is safe to open all places of amusement... Forget all about the 'flu. Come to the Empress to be amused and you will feel

one hundred per cent better than you have during the past six weeks.[15]

That little enjoinment might serve as one of the worst examples of the media placing enterprise above the public good; the flu epidemic was persisting and gatherings such as movie crowds helped spread the virus further.[16]

Before the influenza outbreak, serials – beginning in 1909 and lasting some 45 years – were a popular draw for theatres. Shown traditionally in 20-minute segments sandwiched between the cartoon and the feature presentation, serials kept their fans coming back weekly to keep up with the story. The first American serial was *Les Miserables*; the last was *Blazing the Overland Trail*. While serials were generally shown in 10 or 12 chapters, others went on longer; *The Hazards of Helen* ran in 119 chapters from November 1914 to February 1917, requiring three actresses in the title role. In 1918, five Hollywood serials graced the screen: *A Fight for Millions*, *A Woman in the Web*, *Iron Test*, *Lure of the Circus* and *Wolves of Kultur*. While it's not known what serial played during the flu epidemic, fans at the Empress were able to pick up where they had left off in October so no episodes were missed.

Bowker, sticking with tried-and-true fare, ensured the Empress was busy well into 1919. Movies, concerts and traveling performances had long served as the theatre's stock-in-trade and, as its seventh birthday approached, these standbys were still putting bums in Empress seats. If chatty patrons, crying babies and cellphones are the bane of the modern-day film buff, it appears late arrivals were a test of Bowker's patience that year. As he prepared to present *The Unpardonable Sin* on Wednesday and Thursday, July 23 and 24, Bowker wrote an impassioned plea, printed in the *Macleod News*, to the town to be on time for the curtain. And who would want to be late? The movie, starring Blanche Sweet, Edwin Stevens and Wallace Beery, told the story of how, at the outbreak of the First World War, a mother and one of her two daughters were captured and "debased at the hands of the Germans."[17] The film is not today listed among the best films of 1919.

Said Bowker in his address to *News* readers:

It is not necessary for me to enter into any eulogy of this picture here, but I am taking this means of trying to impress upon those who intend to see this wonderful picture, and that means almost everyone, the necessity of being seated BEFORE the picture starts. You cannot possibly fully enjoy a picture of this kind unless you see it from the very beginning... If you cannot get to the theatre [on time] Wednesday, you will be well advised to wait until Thursday and arrange to arrive in good time. There will be but one show each night and it will start at eight sharp. TRY TO BE ON TIME for this occasion.[18]

In 1919, Bowker secured the Empress as a stop on vaudeville's Hippodrome Circuit – the word Hippodrome derived from the Greek word hippo (horse) and drome (race or course). In ancient Greece, a hippodrome was a stadium used to stage horse and chariot races, highly entertaining events of the times. A flood of theatres in the 1900s bore the title Hippodrome and became showplaces for vaudeville featuring the performance of a wide variety of acts. Several circuits operated in North America during vaudeville's high times, each one developing bills of entertainment that followed a predetermined schedule of performances that made the most of time on the road or perhaps, more accurately, on the tracks. Such schedules remained flexible enough to allow for the insertion of stops at smaller venues such as the Empress while journeying between larger centres.

Bowker again took up his pen to assure customers they would be treated to the best the stage had to offer:

In securing the Hippodrome Circuit the Management of the Empress Theatre realized that it would be useless to bring anything but the best class of Vaudeville to Macleod if the patronage was to be maintained throughout the season. Therefore, the cost of bringing this circuit was only a secondary consider[ation], the first and foremost being the Quality. This it can be truthfully stated is of the highest order as every act that will appear here is identically the same that plays in

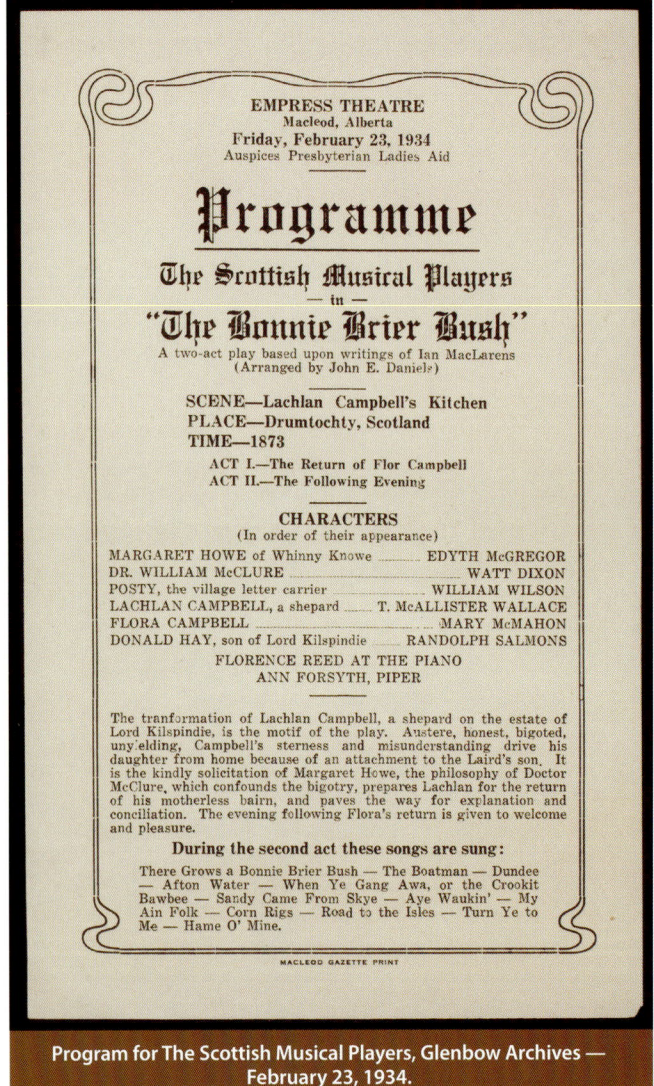

**Program for The Scottish Musical Players, Glenbow Archives — February 23, 1934.**

most of the large western towns and cities in the United States and also from one end of Canada to the other.[19]

And, with a harmonized comment of its own, the *News* weighed in on the Hippodrome entertainment:

> [Hippodrome] is one of the best variety shows that have been given in Macleod for many a long day...this week's program is par excellence. We congratulate the manager of the local theatre on his being able to secure such a splendid vaudeville show and we heartily recommend these programs to the Macleod people.[20]

Ironically for the Empress and for any other North American theatre featuring vaudeville and cinema, the latter hastened the demise of the former. The public's infatuation with movies began to overshadow the popularity of live stage acts. Performers yearned for a place in the Hollywood sun, with its larger salaries and without the need for long-distance traveling. Still, both genres cohabited at the Empress successfully throughout 1919 and 1920. In an advertisement, Bowker explained to his patrons how he had lowered the adult reserved price two bits from 75 cents, hoping to increase attendance:

> Commencing tonight, there will be no seats reserved for the Hippodrome Vaudeville which is at the Empress every Thursday night. This means that you can get the best seat in the house for fifty cents. When one considers that for this small outlay, one can see five excellent reels of pictures and a good clean bill of vaudeville... there is no reason why everybody should not be able to enjoy this form of amusement.[21]

Well, almost everybody; some portions of the community might have held less ardour for the performance of July 8, 1930. Mac Sennett's *Bathing Beauties* graced the Empress stage, and while it is unstated how many attended, any blame for a low turnout of the town's menfolk could not be laid at the feet of the *Times*, which previewed the show with gusto:

> There are blondes and brunettes, practically uniform as to their size and possess the shapeliness necessary to set off their bathing costumes... the young ladies make their appearance in person clad in sporting costumes, in which they give a song and dance and with each song scantier costumes are presented until they reach the bathing suit chorus when the girls appear in some daring effects.[22]

*Bathing Beauties* was likely not the type of stage performance that would delight audiences more used to church productions which often played at the Empress. The Methodist Amateur Theatrical Company shared the theatre with groups from the Anglican, Presbyterian and Catholic churches. Scotch concerts, featuring all manner of local Scottish musical entertainment and tied into Robbie Burns nights, were also popular at the Empress. The 1918 version raised some $300 for disabled soldiers.[23]

The slow capitulation of vaudeville and the rise of the cinema is a "new media" revolution repeated at least twice since. While the movie industry remains relatively strong, it had to weather the rise of television, with entertainment beamed free, apart from the cost of the TV set, into living rooms across the continent. Traditional movie theatres, meanwhile, were unable to escape unscathed from the development of the movie rental business, which itself has undergone transformations from VHS tape to DVD to computer download. Many stars entering vaudeville in its later stages were quick to understand the future offered by cinema, and several soon made the transition.

It is reasonable to assume, too, that managers of the Empress, like those everywhere, realized the cost of bringing in movies was far lower than paying for vaudeville presentations, thus maximizing profit. Worse lay ahead for this live art form with the advent of talking movies:

> The 1930s,... with standardized film distribution and talking pictures,... only confirmed the end of the genre. By 1930, the vast majority of theatres had been wired for sound and none of the major studios was producing silent pictures. For a time, the most luxurious theatres continued to offer live entertainment but the majority of theatres were forced by the Depression to economize.[24]

As noted, film kicked vaudeville to the stage door. Its stars were defecting to Hollywood, and the public's fascination with movies was growing. Once films developed the ability to add sound, they became a complete form of entertainment. Although producers had been experimenting with "talkies" for some years, the first feature film to offer sound, *The Jazz Singer*, was released in 1927. The sound was produced on disc by Vitaphone, then the leading manufacturer of sound-to-disc recordings. A short time later, sound-to-film technology made "talkies" the Hollywood standard. The ripples were felt in Macleod, where the Empress, which had featured Hippodrome Vaudeville almost weekly, began cutting back in favour of films.

The first "talkie" shown at the Empress on November 14, 1929 was *Gold Diggers of Broadway*. The screening at the Empress was the film's premiere showing in Alberta. The *Times* was euphoric:

**Vaudeville show poster, Glenbow Archives — May 16, 1934.**

Unbounded success was the universal pronouncement of the first showing of "talkies" The house was filled to capacity to greet the innovation, and the huge audience was not only delighted with the picture but also with the clearness of the enunciation, especially in the singing. [The picture was] full the equal of like portrayals shown in the largest cities.[25]

*Gold Diggers of Broadway* is historically important as the second all-talking feature-length movie filmed in colour, after *The Desert Song*. *Gold Diggers*, a musical comedy, is notable for giving the world the song *Tiptoe Through the Tulips*, sung by "Crooning Troubadour" Nick Lucas, who starred in the film; the song hit the top of the charts in May 1929.[26]

While the advent of "cheap Tuesdays" and seniors discounts were still decades away, the Empress, as Jobs Thompson explains in her thesis, appeared to have a sliding scale for price of admission based on the type of show presented. Advertisements for Empress productions clearly delineated between live performances and motion pictures. For a popular live act, admission prices ranged from seventy-five cents to one dollar and fifty cents. Other live shows had prices from fifty cents to one dollar. A screen farce might have a price of thirty-five cents plus tax and a photoplay twenty-five cents for adults and ten cents for children.[27]

In 1921, Nellie McClung, one of Canada's "Famous Five" who fought for women's suffrage, was elected as a Liberal member in the Alberta Legislature, and Irene Parlby became the first woman in Alberta to serve as a cabinet minister. At the Empress, "ladies'" admission for a dance, held the year before these breakthroughs, was 50 cents, while men were charged a dollar. Obviously, equality had yet to be achieved at the box office.[28]

Bowker continued his successful four-year run as Empress manager until August 1920 when, quite suddenly, he left for British Columbia. Unlike the relationship between his predecessor and Empress owner Martin, Bowker's tenure seems to have been a smooth one. He was replaced by a member of the theatre's orchestra, Fred C. Cutler, who, after announcing a price increase in September, began to rely more on movies to fill seats with movies such as Charlie Chaplin's *The Kid, The Hustler, The Ace of Hearts, The Adventures of Tarzan, The Sheik* and *The Blot*. The advent of the Academy Awards was still eight years away.

**U.F.A. RALLY**

For South-Western Alberta

Empress Theatre, Macleod

**Wed., Sept. 27th**

Meetings at 2:30 and 7:30 p

**Speeches on C.C.F.**

and other matters of U.F.A. interest.

**SPEAKERS:**

HON. R. G. REID, Provincial Treasurer
E. J. GARLAND, M.P.
GEORGE G. COOTE, M.P.
W. H. SHIELD, M.L.A.
MRS. H. B. MACLEOD, U.F.W.A. Director
A. SMEATON, M.L.A., and others.

We are anxious to make this Rally an outstanding success.
EVERYBODY IS INVITED.          COME IF YOU CAN.

UFA Rally Poster, Glenbow Archives — September 27, 1933.

**50 - VOICES - 50**

THE LETHBRIDGE
**MALE VOICE CHOIR**

under the auspices of

**THE MACLEOD WOMEN'S INSTITUTE**

will hold a Grand

**CONCERT**

--- at the ---

**EMPRESS THEATRE, MACLEOD**
**WEDNESDAY, APRIL 26**

Commencing at 8:15 p.m.

This Choir of Fifty Voices is recognized as one
of the best vocal aggregations in Western
Canada.   A real musical treat.

General Admission **35c** ----- Children **25c**

Poster for concert by Lethbridge Male Voice Choir, Glenbow Archives —
April 26, 1934.

CHAPTER SIX

# ONE OF THE MOST UP-TO-DATE TALKIE HOUSES IN THE PROVINCE.

*FRED CUTLER sat in his office located in the front of the Empress and pondered his frustration. He enjoyed his role as musician at the Empress – always had – and was keen to take over from Bowker as manager. Running the theatre would provide him a challenge, one that would stretch his abilities beyond a deft touch with violin and bow. Lately, though, the violin remained in its case while Cutler instead fiddled with Empress paperwork. Sometimes he admitted it was more than he bargained for.*

*Can you believe, he thought, these performance contracts? Our little orchestra simply walks on stage and plays. Not these big-city folk, though, oh, no. They come into our little Empress for six nights and matinees, and don't they want the moon? And me running the place and trying to keep Martin off my back. So, reading this contract, they want the Empress* "well lighted, cleaned and heated." *Well, what did they think they were going to get, dim, dirty and dank? I rather think not; hardly at the Empress. And listen to this fine and fancy legal twaddle:* "with all the requisited attaches." *I'm a musician, not a lawyer; maybe Martin should run his own theatre.*

"Electric light connections on stage, stage furniture, necessary stage hands." *Yes, yes, OK. Now, what's this?* "Imperishable properties." *What in heaven's name? Bowker would have known that one.* "Scenery and equipment;" *yes, OK. Then they want house programmes, coupon tickets, bill posting, billboards – billboards? – distributing and hanging. Oh, there will be a hanging, all right; I'll knock up the scaffold myself. Advertising in advance and throughout the run. Maybe they don't understand we have weekly newspapers here in Macleod. And would you listen to this mumbo jumbo:* "to receive all baggage, scenery and properties, on the arrival of the company at the stage door, and to carefully carry same to all dressing and property rooms, and stage; and to take the same from dressing, property rooms and stage and deliver outside of stage door immediately after last performance ending such engagement, FREE." *Free in capital letters, no less, and* "…employ sufficient stage hands to properly handle party of the first part's scenery…"

*Oh, dear, oh, dear, oh dear: does anyone wonder why we are running more movies these days? Well, at least our patrons will be entertained by six acts. That should fill seats. And the company agrees to pay its travel expenses, take care of royalties, 10 per cent of the orchestra's salaries, the picture programs and 40 per cent of newspaper advertising. The Empress takes 60 per cent of the gate. Raising film prices was a mistake; I'm going to lower them to 30 cents for adults and 12½ cents for kiddies. We run a good, clean operation with appropriate films and a musical setting equal to those of many city houses. But Macleod has a much smaller population. If more people don't show up, I can't retain those standards. Perhaps I should say as much in the* Times.

Cutler's thoughts are conjecture, but details of the contract, taken from a standard agreement of the day between traveling company and theatre, are accurate.[1] And, Cutler was relying on movies more as his stock in trade. His son Jack recalls his father changing the movies up to three times a week, most of which the younger Cutler availed himself. Jack remembers, though, once in 1924 when his father kept *The Covered Wagon* running all week. The movie, starring J. Warren Kerrigan, Lois Wilson and Alan Hale, father of Alan Hale Jr., the "Skipper" on the TV series *Gilligan's Island*, recounted the daunting trip settlers were forced to make to reach Oregon, spiced with a love story and requisite attacks by movie "Indians." Cutler ran the film continuously from morning to midnight. Young Jack, who helped around the Empress, avowed he "swept more peanut shells in that theatre those mornings than I am sure have been seen in that town since."[2] It is not known why *The Covered Wagon* so entranced Macleod's movie fans, although a rollicking western was likely a pretty good draw back then, especially in a prairie community; at least it sold peanuts.

Two years after *The Covered Wagon* finally lumbered out of town, the Empress turned 14, and Cutler decided she needed a sprucing. The work, which lasted several years, began with interior painting and redecorating. Although details were not recorded in the local press, the *Macleod Times* opened on August 26, 1926: "the local theatre certainly looks fine now."

Sadly, Empress owner Martin had died of the complications of diabetes that May, just 55 years old, leaving the building to his wife Ruby. (Interestingly, Martin had been one of the first patients to be treated with that most notable of Canadian discoveries: insulin; a dose was sent to him by its discoverer, Dr. Frederick Banting.)[3]

Likely unprepared to run the theatre on her own, Ruby Martin sold it to Augustus T. Leather, a prominent Macleod businessman and one-time chairman of the Macleod Hospital Board who was likely well known to her late husband.[4] Leather was a real estate broker who held considerable property in the community and surrounding area; as a month's time would prove, he had purchased the Empress for its speculative value. The sale was reported in the *Times* on September 13, 1928, indicating a fair price had been reached between Leather and Ruby Martin, and that the purchaser was already erecting a brick building on the lot immediately east of the Empress.

Photo Courtesy: Trevor Anderson

Service men and women from #2 Flying Instructor School (BCATP), Pearce, Alberta performed at the Empress in a December 1944 variety show. Photo courtesy of Trevor Anderson. His mother, Vera (Powell) Anderson – RCAF Women's Division/Pearce air training station/accounts receivable men's mess — appears front row, 7th from left.

A month later, Leather sold the Empress to two entrepreneurs, James A. Booth and William Beatty from Indian Head, Saskatchewan who owned theatres elsewhere, as readers of the *Times* were to learn: "The new owners have theatres at Indian Head, Lloydminster and Calgary, and a brother of Mr. Beatie [sic] owns the theatre at Red Deer, so they control a chain of theatres."[5] When Beatty and Booth arrived in Macleod the following month, the *Times* noted they had "a wide experience in the movie game, which will doubtless be an asset in their catering to Macleod patrons of the silver screen."[6]

It undoubtedly was. Booth and Beatty appear to have turned the Empress almost exclusively into a movie theatre. The press ceased any mention of live theatre, except for local productions, and movies became the pair's standard fare, especially with the advent of "talkies."

*The Wind*, *The Crowd* and *The Cameraman* all entertained audiences in 1928, and the inaugural best picture Oscar (1927-28) went to *Wings*, shown again at the Empress 82 years later for a special tribute to the Commonwealth Air Training Plan in November 2010 with Dennis James playing organ throughout the silent film. Not content to merely run the theatre as they found it, Booth and Beatty soon embarked on a renovation project that would significantly change the look of the Empress. Work on the interior included the replacement of older drop curtains at the stage front with new black sateen draw curtains displaying advertisements of local firms. The orchestra pit was fitted with decorative curtains and the lobby adorned with coloured lights. As well, plans included ornamental panels for the walls.

The *Times* submitted that the "theatre will present a decorative appearance second to none" in the area and reports the proprietors' belief that the "steadily increasing patronage" shows that theatre goers appreciate their efforts.[7] A month later, the *Times* commented on the "wall decorations... in development" saying that, when finished, they will "make the Macleod theatre one of the most... attractive amusement places in Southern Alberta."

The Booth-Beatty partnership didn't enjoy a long run at the Empress. In June 1929, Beatty sold his interest in the theatre to Cecil J. Hughes of Neepawa, Manitoba, who had been working for some time as the theatre's projectionist.[8] Hughes and

> HUGHES AND BOOTH WERE OBVIOUSLY BETTING ON THE FUTURE, THOUGH THEY COULD HARDLY KNOW THE EXTENT OF THE RISK.

James Booth, more familiarly known as Alf, were prepared to lavish money on improvements to the Empress. Chief among these was updated sound equipment, a development allowing the introduction of talking motion pictures to Macleod, while ushering out almost all forms of traveling performances.

A great film shown on poor equipment in a first-rate theatre, as the Empress now was, is still disappointing. Advancements in film projection were ongoing with shaper lenses, sound, and camera movement. Originally, cameras were hand-cranked, shooting film at varied speeds producing varied results when projected in theatres. With the advent of "talkies," a constant speed was required to synchronize the action with the sound.

The "talkie" era began at the Empress November 14, some two weeks after Black Friday, the collapse of the American stock market. Booth and Hughes basically bet the house that "talkies" would make their theatre financially stable. The local newspapers were again onboard, informing readers of the renovation's wonders and rating the Empress among the best in Alberta.[9]

A week prior to the launch of sound, the *Macleod Times* described the changes, from a double front designed to shut out street noise and to "prevent draughts to those occupying back seats." The *Times* extolled the sound equipment as the best on the market able to accommodate Movietone and Vitaphone films, and praised the visual proponent as being equal to any used in city theatres. Canadians who went to movies between 1929 and 1979 likely saw a British Movietone News reel. Vitaphone was the brand name for the process of recording sound onto vinyl disks and synchronizing it to the film.

The Empress owners installed two new projectors, along with a "rotary converter" to produce sharper pictures, and installed new matting to damp the sound of footfalls. Crowed the *Times*:

These improvements are on the biggest scale ever made in this theatre and the management are to be congratulated on having faith in Macleod and district to invest the huge sum necessary to make such elaborate improvements. It is hoped that the public will appreciate these efforts and take advantage of having a theatre on a city scale right in their own town and give it their hearty support.[10]

Such unabashed media support for a lone business would be virtually impossible to enlist today, especially when it involves chiding the public.

Another indicator of expected prosperity, a new $500 neon sign ordered months earlier was installed in March 1930, even though the Great Depression was about to bookmark a decade in which two-thirds of farmers in the Palliser Triangle were forced onto government aid and many others left for urban areas. But all that was in the near future. The flickering neon, introduced to North America just seven years before, was regarded by the *Times* as yet another grand improvement to keep the Empress "abreast of the times regarding equipment as well as productions – one of the most up-to-date Talkie houses in the province."[11]

Hughes and Booth were obviously betting on the future, though they could hardly know the extent of the risk. The lobby was repainted. Opulent green carpeting was laid there and down the aisles. Walls were painted rose pink, trimmed with gold panels. Again, the *Times* gushed: "The effect is extremely pleasing, and the management is to be complimented on their initiative in keeping the Macleod Theatre abreast of all the playhouses in Alberta."[12]

Monarchies can be expensive to maintain; Booth and Hughes were about to discover, as the Depression loomed, that keeping the Empress was perhaps above their ability to pay. Town wags noted the Empress's proprietors were not without their tastes for fun and frivolity, as signs of a weakening economy became apparent. Besides the parties they managed to throw, the pair leased the Highwood Theatre in High River in March 1931, despite waning business in Macleod.[13] In May, they cut movie nights at the Empress to three per week, as profits from Monday to Wednesday were less than scintillating. The *Macleod Gazette* was moved to opine: "Theatre patrons will regret this change, as ...Booth and Hughes have been giving excellent theatre service to Macleod, and it is hoped that the change will not be of long duration."[14]

It wasn't. By September, fare at the Empress was again offered six nights a week.[15] But the cut in service was the canary in the coal mine signaling the Depression was ramping up for a long run, and extra pocket money for frivolities such as movies was running scarce. To encourage patrons to pull out that spare change, theatres across North America had to be creative. All today's movie fan really expects, besides an engaging film, is a generous splash of melted butter on the popcorn. In 1931, however, theatres had to go a little further. Some offered free coffee and gum to patrons waiting in the lobbies. Others gave away premiums, much like the gifts stuffed in detergent boxes years later, or the tumbler giveaways at gas stations. Freebies such as glassware, silverware and cash were offered as prizes in a game called Hollywood in which a wheel of fortune was projected on the screen and players had a shot at $20 in winnings.

Booth and Hughes perhaps reached their zenith in this enterprise late in the year when their advertisement in the *Macleod Gazette* announced the commencement of Ladies' Silverware Night, a unique and long-term come-on enticing women to attend on Monday nights when they would "receive free one piece of table silverware." A single spoon might not be sufficient encouragement to leave the house on a chilly Monday evening, but the two entrepreneurs saw well beyond that first week: "Be sure to attend the first night so you can start from the beginning and get the full set of 52 pieces...."

No sooner had Ladies' Silverware Night taken wing, Booth and Hughes took a grand step further in enticing patrons to their movies: the pair closed the Empress for three days to install an upgraded sound system to replace the disc system.[16] Recall, the older system carried the film's soundtrack on a disc, much like a phonograph record. Because the disc ran independently of the film, the opportunity for the two to run out of synch was great whenever the stylus skipped. The new system recorded the soundtrack directly onto the film, thus ensuring synchronicity.

Those ladies who began their silverware collections in November 1931 fell far short of the full 52 pieces. Free cutlery and movie sound "seldom found outside of the cities"[17] couldn't outrun the winds of the Depression, and the sagging fortunes of the theatre business soon forced Booth and Hughes into financial assignment. Three days before Christmas, the pair was forced to give way to British Canadian Trust of Lethbridge. As the *Gazette* explained in its January 7, 1932 edition, the Empress, the only theatre still operating in Macleod, was to be operated by the former management, with Neville Kirk, BCT's representative, watching over their shoulders.[18]

> THE DEPRESSION WAS ABOUT TO SET IN, AND TOWN WAGS NOTED THE EMPRESS'S PROPRIETORS WERE NOT WITHOUT THEIR TASTES FOR FUN AND FRIVOLITY.

The move bought Hughes and Booth but a few days. Creditors soon determined financial prudence dictated the Empress be closed indefinitely, its doors shut before the month was out. They would remain shuttered for eight months, during which time the Empress, in just the 20th year of her reign, was paraded through bankruptcy court in Lethbridge, a shoddy way for royalty to be treated. The Empress's fate wasn't an isolated case, however. The early 1930s were not what Hollywood would refer to now as banner financial years. In *Show Biz from Vaude to Video*, the authors note sentiments often expressed about Hollywood today:

> [The box office], crippled by the depression, was hit equally hard by public charges that the films being made were lemons and the stars grossly overpaid. Film attendance dropped 40 per cent, forcing cuts in studio and theatre overhead. Bankers, previously lenient with the industry, began to demand more concrete collateral – and the only collateral producers could offer was the diminishing interest of the public in films...[19]

Even with declining revenues, the film industry's product was not all bad: 1930 produced *All Quiet on the Western Front*, a superb anti-war film focusing on the horrors of the First World War, while the Marx Brothers offered up *Animal Crackers*; 1931 arrived with the boxing drama *The Champ*, and Charlie Chaplin in *City Lights*. For horror fans, Bela Legosi donned a cape for *Dracula* and Boris Karloff epitomized the monster in *Frankenstein*. Katherine Hepburn starred in 1932's *A Bill of Divorcement*, and Mae West spoke on film for the first time in *Night After Night*.

But at the Empress, the horror show dragged on, unfolded to the public on the pages of the *Gazette*. In May, Mr. Justice Tweedie, the Lethbridge judge who had heard bankruptcy arguments informally two months earlier, issued a formal ruling that freed British Canadian Trust to dispose of the theatre as it saw fit; it saw fit to sell it. Clarence L. Downsley, a Lethbridge theatre manager, had an agreement with Booth and Hughes to operate the Empress. He then sued British Canadian Trust to allow him to operate the Empress, but his lawsuit and subsequent appeal were rejected by Alberta courts.[20]

This opened the door for the reappearance, after a four-year absence, of Augustus Leather, the Macleod speculator who listed on the title his wife Jessie Gertrude Marshall Leather. Augustus Leather then rented the Empress to R. A. Clement, owner of Macleod's Rexall Drug Store, and Daniel Boyle, owner of Granum's Starland Theatre (thus making Boyle the first manager in Empress history to be referred to in the press by his full first name)[21]. Boyle's involvement, though brief the first time around, would prove to be a harbinger of what might well be termed the "golden age" of the Empress.

Boyle and Clement reopened the Empress September 1, 1932 with a showing of *The Shanghai Express*, starring Marlene Dietrich, an event the *Gazette* predicted would be met with "considerable pleasure" by local theatregoers. Through the first two months of 1933, while a related lawsuit was being heard by the Supreme Court (the action was dismissed in mid-October),[22] the Empress opened Thursdays to Saturdays only, but by March it was again in full six-night swing. The rest of the year and a good portion of 1934 passed with the drama confined to the stage in local theatre productions and on screen.

Then in August, the bankrupt Alf Booth made an encore. Teaming with R. L. Holm, whom the *Gazette* described as being associated with theatres in Red Deer and Stettler, Booth again ascended to the Empress's front office. As before, Booth felt the need to keep the Empress abreast of technological improvements, including a new projection-room amplifier, loud speaker and screen. The improvements, as usual, caused excitement in the *Gazette* newsroom: "With these installations, both the vision and the sound have been improved, and the showings in this theatre will be second to none."[23]

Perhaps. However, a better security system might have been a more expeditious expenditure, because sometime on the night of April 29-30, 1935, the Empress again fell victim to burglary. It didn't take a master thief to raise the street-side window, enter the theatre's office, rifle through drawers to find, and make off with $20 in change. The *Gazette*, pointing out the only bright spot in the situation, reported, "The door receipts for Monday evening's show were not in the theatre, and therefore the amount realized by the thieves was not as large as they probably had expected."[24]

The middle years of the decade blew past, along with most of the prairie's topsoil. In Hollywood, movies were still being made and anointed with Best Picture Oscars. Following 1934's *It Happened One Night, Mutiny on the Bounty* won in 1935; the musical *The Great Ziegfeld* won in 1936 and *The Life of Emile Zola* was tops in 1937. In Macleod, The Life of Dan Boyle was about to be premiered.

CHAPTER SEVEN

# I KNOW NOTHING ABOUT RUNNING TALKING PICTURES.

DAN BOYLE might well have quietly given thanks for the good sense to build with brick as he surveyed the remains of downtown Granum the morning following the fire in July 1934. The blaze had razed an entire block, but had spared the Boyle Building, an office block that housed a butcher shop, a men's store, drug store and barber shop. The day was fast approaching when Granum would be mined out in terms of economic growth and Boyle would be forced to look beyond its limits, something he felt reluctant to do. He had arrived in Granum as a kid in 1909. During the years, he had fallen in love with the place; later, he had fallen in love there as well.

But now, he was a family man; Edna and the little ones deserved the best he could give them. The Starland in Granum had been a grand opportunity, teaching him what he needed to know about running a theatre, but now was the time to consider his financial future. Lethbridge might have seemed more than he wanted to take on at 41, but Macleod was a pleasant community and the Empress was a first-class facility that could turn a penny if run properly. He'd come to know the Empress intimately during his brief time there back in 1932 as co-manager. Likely, he and Edna discussed the move at length and, as a true man of the art, he no doubt saw himself in that snug lobby greeting patrons as they arrived for a premiere. Four years later, and two years after the Granum fire, he made his move. He returned as sole proprietor, purchasing the Empress from Leather and vowing to maintain the level of service Empress patrons had enjoyed in the past. He went far beyond this promise.

Before that promise showed itself, Boyle had learned from previous experience. Born in New Brunswick, Dan Boyle was 12 when his family, including two older brothers and a sister, moved to the new province of Alberta in 1905. His father James worked as a carpenter and as a mine engineer. Dan was schooled in Blairmore and later moved with the family to Granum. He and his brother Stanley homesteaded near Foremost, living in a shack so cold at night that Stanley claimed once quilts and coats were piled on the bed, Dan would add a saddle for warmth. Taught the violin by a cousin, Dan earned money playing at dances, while the brothers struggled to work their land.[1]

Dan eventually moved back to Granum to work in an elevator before he and his brother joined the army to serve in the First World War. Dan survived a bout of the Spanish flu in 1918 and, upon recovering, purchased the Granum Opera House. It was here he steeped himself in all aspects of theatre operations, running the community's lone source of entertainment. During his early years in Granum, Boyle presented movies, dances and the annual Chautauqua, a traveling tent show originating in Chautauqua Lake, N.Y.

Boyle was actively involved in the community. As Mary Yvonne (Boyle) Dunne writes, her father, at the age of 25, was "...considered a catch. He had one of the first cars in town and could be seen driving down main street, smoking a cigar and somehow he had his leg hanging out the car window."[2] As a member of the Granum Dramatic Society in the 1930s, Dan helped produce and act in skits put on by the Elks Club.

It's likely he and his future wife Edna Swanson first developed a fondness for each other while on stage in the dramatic society's production of *A Pair of Sixes* in January 1930. Beyond his natural charm, Boyle might well have piqued Edna's interest with the humour he infused in his letters to her, after she moved to Lethbridge to teach school:

> Say Edna your judgment about those old time dances was sure correct. I was silly enough to go last Monday to one and it was the gosh awfulest affair I was ever at. Some of those old boys would barge down the centre of the little hall and when they got through they would leave a trail of wounded and dying in their wake. Of course they parked their guns outside but still I left the dance firmly convinced that dancing is a very rough sport.[3]

In Granum during the 1930s, Boyle was a one-man operation. He could install and operate new equipment as it arrived, as well as repair and improve existing equipment, often running between his operations in Claresholm and Stavely to handle such responsibilities as they arose. In a charming collection of letters he wrote to Edna as they were courting during the first half of 1930, Boyle described the economy when Granum, like the rest of the nation, was hit hard by the Depression:

> Things are mighty-mighty quiet in this here town of our'n. Although I had a pretty good day in the store today. I pretty near sold a fellow a suit of clothes, and another fellow I very nearly sold a hat to. Of course on an average, business doesn't keep up as good as that. But you can see there is money in this business. How do I know? Well Ain't I put plenty in it?[4]

Other letters revealed his triumphs and frustrations as he attempted to secure and install the equipment necessary to accommodate talking pictures in his Granum operation:

> I have to go to Claresholm tonight as Mr. Milnes wants me to 'add color' to his show. He has no second class projectionist there and the theatre inspector was going to close his theatre if he did not get one at once and as I happen to have one, he wanted me to go up for a while till he gets one. I don't see what use I will be to him as I know nothing about running talking pictures.[5]

His self-described shortcoming regarding the knowledge of talking film was soon laid to rest; Granum was about to be treated to this latest technological leap. Again, Edna was kept up to date throughout May in almost daily letters from her betrothed:

> I expect my talkie equipment will arrive about next Friday or Saturday. It was shipped from Winnipeg on the eighth of May. So expect for the next week or so after that, all will be confusion with me. Guess I'll try and get up some of the curtains next week to see how they look.[6]

Later:

> Received your nice letter this a.m. I am writing this letter up home and with the darndest pen in captivity. Had another busy day. Believe me dear I don't find any trouble in getting to sleep these nights, and will henceforth prescribe work as a sure cure for all ailments. Am going back tonight after supper and take another whirl at it. Most of the equipment has arrived but I am still short a few things which are necessary for good talkers.[7]

> Just a few lines tonight before the show. Have been working today (as usual) on the blinking talking equipment and honestly dear I can hardly see what I have done, there is so darn much to be done yet. I have now three picture machines in the booth and there is no room to move around in it. But I have to keep the old one in till after tonight and then I am going to hook up at least one of the others for Friday and Saturday.[8]

After the May long weekend, he writes:

> Have just had my supper and will take this opportunity of writing a few lines in my perfect English heh heh!!

and a couple of ho hums! It's what I should have done last night but I planned on being finished work at about nine o clock and writing you then. But to keep a long story that way, I worked till half past twelve. Emil Kern helped me and we had plenty of hard luck. I have a cut on each hand so don't take any notice of this punk writing. It's no worse than usual at that. I received your letter this morning dearest, the one written in school and also the one I should have gotten on Friday. Thanks for both. I am going back to work again tonight and at the present rate of speed I expect I will have the talkies fully installed and working in 1932, if all is well.[9]

And in late May:

> Well dearest I tried out the rigging last night. I got down a couple of reels from Calgary, they were not exactly talking pictures, just music and singing, but the strangest part is, it worked. I wish I had a picture with talk in it, as you can't tell yet whether you will be able to hear voices plain or not. However it won't be long now until I do know. I work every night now and it always seems as if I actually accomplish more after supper, than during the day. I think I will get May and Mother to come down tonight and see the two reels I have and see what they think of it.[10]

In June, he continued to provide Edna with the blow-by-blow details:

> Well dear today is the third of June and my birthday. Incidentally it's King George's [V] too. I am just beginning to find out that it's the little details in completing the theatre for the talkies which take the time. I am still working at it and have plenty to do yet. I painted the booth today. It's a bottle green and sure is dark. But it has to be a dark color. I was telling Emil

---

**BOYLE AND THE EMPRESS GREW TOGETHER, EMBRACING THE TECHNOLOGIES THAT, DURING THE 1930S, '40S AND '50S, COMPRISED THE QUANTUM LEAPS OF FILMMAKING**

---

last night that the booth looked a lot smaller when painted dark. But I guessed there would be just as much room in it, and Emil agreed that it would not cut down the size any. He wasn't kidding either! Well dear it won't be long now until I know whether the talkies are going to be okay or a big flop, and after that I will turn all of my attention to weeding the garden and seeing about the house and in short, planning on our future.[11]

And:

> Just a line before the show sweetheart. Say dear the recording on the Hoot Gibson picture last night was as good as any I ever heard, it came in fine. But the picture itself was not so hot and the comedy was the bunk. In the first reel of the talking comedy we had our first taste of getting out of synk. We stopped and put on a new disk and everything was fine, it only took a minute. Well sweet it's getting closer to our big Day, not much over two weeks, now.[12]

Finally, as wedding plans came down to the wire, Boyle wrote on June 20:

> Last night we screened The Cocoanuts and had plenty of trouble with it. There were three reels out of synk. So don't know what is going to happen tonight. I have a bet of 60 cents up with Butch that it won't go out of synk tonight.[13]

Dan and Edna were married on July 7, 1930. The newlyweds made Granum their home. Their son Neil, who would have his own act to play in the Empress story, was born the following year, joined by a daughter Mary Yvonne in 1934.

By mid-decade Boyle had 18 years of theatre operation experience and was ready for change. Under his management, the Granum theatre had enjoyed close to two decades of stability, whereas the theatre in Macleod went through nine changes of management during the same period; while the Empress made headlines, the Starland made money. Boyle's accomplishment is not surprising taking into account his considerable abilities, aided by a keen sense of humour "which even the knottiest of problems could not subdue."[14] His elan could not help but translate into success at the Empress as well.

When limit to Granum's growth became apparent and Boyle had moved to Macleod, the new manager was quick to implement change. A self-taught projectionist, he kept the Empress open six days, changed movies three times a week and offered two showings per night. He used French doors and glass to close in the arched exterior vestibule, creating more lobby space for patrons who previously had to line up on Twenty-fourth Street (now Main Street) exposed to the predations of weather, chiefly the west wind. Renovations also afforded washrooms and a concession.

Boyle had the orchestra pit removed and a new curved stage front installed. He moved the projection room upstairs, changed the heating system to steam and brought in air conditioning. This "swamp-cooler" air conditioning helped the Empress become the coolest place around during hot summers, and many theatre patrons sat through two showings of the same movie just to avoid returning to the blast furnace of the street. Swamp coolers use the principle of evaporation to create cold airflow, as opposed to chemically charged air conditioners; they're popular, and work best in hot, dry climates such as southern Alberta's. The one Dan Boyle installed was removed in the major theatre renovation in 1988.[15]

Boyle installed "loveseats," or double-wide seats, creating, along with witty comments for the next six decades, a staggered seating plan that allowed for relatively unobstructed views of the stage. Story has it Edna was particularly fond of tulips, bouquets of which Dan presented to her each birthday. When he forgot the flowers one year, Boyle was moved to install the Empress's famed neon tulips on the ceiling of the auditorium. Edna, in turn, sewed dark-blue velvet curtains to close off the alcoves.

During the Second World War, Boyle added a 100-seat balcony

Photo: Jaime Vedres

Empress' famed neon tulip graces the original pressed tin ceiling.

to complement the 271 main-floor seats to accommodate increased patronage from the Macleod site of the British Commonwealth Air Training Plan; the balcony was reserved for officers, while enlisted men sat below. Boyle also opened two theatres, one on the Macleod base and a second in the small community of Pearce, two miles from town, home to yet another flight training school. Hundreds of Canadians, British, Australians and New Zealanders went through the school and through the doors of the Empress to enjoy the completely remodeled interior with its plush red carpets, washrooms off the lobby, modern glass front doors, carrara (transluscent white) glass around the ticket booth, and a series of large round mirrors adding a shot of showbiz glitz.

Glitz also arrived on foot: Boyle helped bring Rod Cameron, a western movie star, to the Macleod Stampede. Cameron, born Nathan Cox in Calgary, was just two the year the Empress opened. While he played in various action genres, he's best known for his work in westerns and, in an unusual personal twist, for divorcing his wife and marrying her mother.[16]

Boyle also brought comedian Bill Thompson, a star of the radio

Photo Courtesy: Gary Kennedy

**Rod Cameron with local residents
Emily Hatton and Ethel Feeney (1949).**

show *Fibber McGee and Molly*, to the stampede.[17] Thompson actually played four characters on the program, including The Old-Timer, Boomer, Nick Depopulis and Wallace Wimple. Thompson, whose parents were vaudevillians, is best known for his voice-overs in several Disney films, including *Peter Pan*, *Lady and the Tramp* and *The Aristocats*.[18]

In 1953, Boyle invited TV's Robert Stack (*The Untouchables*, *Unsolved Mysteries*) to southern Alberta as his guest during the Fort Macleod Stampede.[19] (The town restored *Fort* to its name earlier that year.) Stack was made an honorary chief of the Peigan Nation, given the name Chief Crow Flag. According to Boyle's daughter, Mary Yvonne, the Hollywood star stayed in the Boyle home and, in an amusing touch of prairie hospitality, shared a bed with Dan.

Boyle and the Empress grew together, embracing the technologies that, during the 1930s, '40s and '50s, comprised the quantum leaps of filmmaking: Technicolor, CinemaScope, surround sound and 3-D. He became Macleod's vicarious link to Hollywood, visiting film lots, meeting movie stars and taking in

the glamour and glitz it offered in large dollops.

Boyle brought to the Empress a spirit of derring-do, a promotional panache that kept the theatre a going concern. Boyle family archivist Mary Yvonne provides insight into the wonderful weirdness her father brought to the front office, much of which spilled onto the street. He combined a head for fanfare and a talent for carpentry to highlight a particular train movie, building and installing a locomotive that appeared to be streaking through the Empress wall. Family recollection records how Dan constructed the locomotive in one of the dressing rooms; when the project was completed, he was forced to remove the door frame to extricate his handiwork. For another promotion, the 1937 opening of *A Star Is Born* starring Fredric March, Boyle built a giant star. When quizzed as to why he had posted another actor's photo in the display, his answer was simple and to him, at least, obvious: "Can't find a picture of Fredric March."[20]

Macleod movie fans, like most others across North America in 1939, were desperate to see Metro-Goldwyn-Mayer's *Gone With The Wind* on the big screen. In the hype leading up to the release, all theatres, the Empress included, were required to sell advance tickets, plan for intermissions and offer matinees. According to Mary Yvonne, he made little money from what was deemed a "percentage picture," on which the distributor took a set slice of the gate. Records donated to the Glenbow Archives in Calgary indicate MGM held a tight rein on how *GWTW* was to be presented, even years later, when Boyle brought it back to

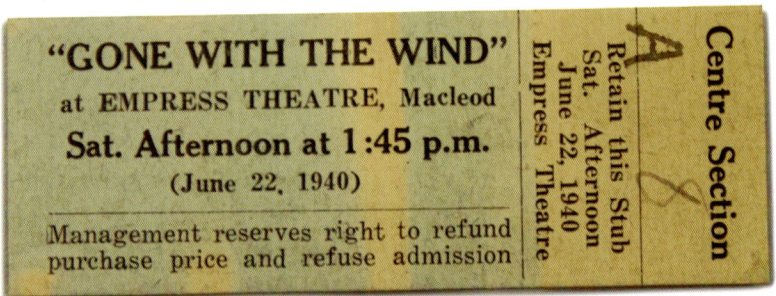

*Gone with the Wind* ticket June 22, 1940 – Empress Theatre collection.

Manager Boyle was required to record each movie's attendance in a box office statement, along with the day's weather. One such report indicates May 9, 1958 was "clear and warm" for a showing of Cecil B. DeMille's *The Ten Commandments*, which drew 96 adults at $1.10; 23 students at 65 cents and 53 children at 50 cents for a total house of 172 and a gate of $147.05. Paramount's terms for the film required Boyle to spend "not less than" $40 for newspaper advertising and $35.60 for "other forms of advertising (the studio did not require any radio or television ads) and agreed to pay 50 per cent of the cost. Again, the contract stipulated Boyle must pay $1.50 for the trailer. The province also required theatres to record and submit amusement tax records accompanied by the amount owing. One such tax record indicates that for April 25, 1953, Boyle cut a cheque for $45.42.[24]

Correspondence from Arthur Hersh, branch manager for Warner Bros. Pictures Distributing Company Ltd. in Calgary, dated December 3, 1954, lays out Boyle's cost for four upcoming releases. For *The High and the Mighty*, set to run on a weekend, Warner would take $225, plus 50 per cent of any gate greater than $675. The other three shows (*Lucky Me*, *Ring of Fear*, *King Richard and the Crusaders*) set to run on weeknights would cost the Empress $150, plus 50 per cent on receipts greater than $450. Hersh included a contract for CinemaScope colour short subjects at $5 per single and $10 per two-reeler.[25]

These numbers may not seem a king's ransom today, but at the time, each ticket, each box of popcorn sold was crucial to the business end of the Empress. While no concession report for the Empress could be located, one exists for an evening at Boyle's Fort Drive-In dated July 3, 1955, listing sales of 40 10-cent and eight 25-cent popcorns; 101 drinks; 49 Revels; six Chiclets; three Lifesavers; 40 hotdogs, a pack of smokes, one cigar, a penny book of matches and assorted other goodies added up to a take of $35.83.[26]

Dan Boyle might have once loved Granum, but the Empress was now his mistress. He had guided the theatre through the end of the Depression and into a period of prosperity. And he wasn't finished yet.

ONE OF
NEW YORK'S *50* MOST BEAUTIFUL SHOW GIRLS
*in* "MOONLIGHT *and* PRETZELS
*Universal's Smash Musical Hit!*

Star card featuring Anya Taranda – actress, show girl, model – dressed for her role in Universal's movie *Moonlight and Pretzels* released in 1933. The card, courtesy Dianne Perrin, is one of a set collected by her grandfather, Blakely McNeil, early projectionist at the Empress.

Anya Taranda

59

Front of theatre showing archway—Town of Fort Macleod Archives, Empress Theatre collection, 1916.

IT WOULD BE REASONABLE to conclude Dan Boyle ran the Empress tight to the bone. In January 1950, he wrote to V. M. Skorey, Twentieth Century Fox's representative in Calgary, seeking reductions in his rental rates since business was hard hit by a particularly miserable winter. Skorey promised to pass Boyle's request to his head office, but held out little hope Boyle would receive relief based on poor weather, over which, noted Skorey, Fox had little control. Skorey wrote:

> It wouldn't be so bad if the extreme weather was confined to one locality and for a short time but it is almost international and it has been prolonged for six weeks.
> I don't suppose it is any consolation to you but, for your information, business has been bad since the second week of December [1949] and the only pictures that I know of that have been doing business at all are PINKY and I WAS A MALE WAR BRIDE (and these are doing outstanding business).[1]

Skorey's head office proved unsympathetic regarding the vagaries of southern Alberta's climate; on March 8, Boyle wrote to MGM's Canadian distribution office in Toronto with a detailed complaint concerning the studio's rental rates. With his frustration likely superseding his attention to spelling and punctuation, Boyle hammered out the following on his keyboard:

> Dear Mr. Gould:
> Since my last letter to you re rentals of Film, and since signing a Contract with Mr. Guss for your product for 1949-50, I have uncovered a few figures which I am sending along to you. My reason for not mentioning these figures before signing the contract with your firm, is because I dident have these figures until very recently which were obtained from my 1949 Income tax return.
> These figures were an eye opener for me, as they show that I paid 40% for Film in 1949. Now Showmen who are a lot more clever than I [am] have shown that a Theatre in a small town such as this cannot afford to pay even 30% for film. I know of course there are exceptions to this, such as Radio City Music Hall in New York, and others. But in a Town such as mine there is only so much business to be done, and that mostly on Saturday Nights and in paying the rentals I paid last year, makes it impossible for me to make any money, and this year of 1950 the rentals are still higher, with Metro in the fold, higher than them all.
> Business is bound to be off some in the coming year, due in part to January and Feby. being so terribly cold that there just wasent any business to speak of in these two months, as a Matter of fact I wrote Metro asking for an adjustment in rental price on three of your pictures played during these two months, but havent heard any word of getting same yet.

CHAPTER EIGHT

# ...IN A TOWN SUCH AS MINE THERE IS ONLY SO MUCH BUSINESS.

Its possible you may be inclined to take my above statement writing Fox, Paramount, R.K.O. and Warners, along with your company. I cant see why the five Companies couldn't get an Auditor to down here and check my last years business and Film rentals, and see for yourselves the business done and Rentals Paid.

The Extremely high Film rentals for my Town have been caused, First by Exchange Managers, presumeably with instructions from head office, insisting on getting increased rentals every year, Secondly, by my insisting on doing away with percentage pictures. (I feel very strongly about percentage pictures in a small town such as Macleod, where Saturday is our big night, and where more often than not we run the first four nights of the week at a loss, and then a picture which is a good draw comes along and Exhibitor pays out in percentage, overage monies he should have to keep his Theatre running, account of bad nights on indifferent pictures) which the Exchanges met and settled by boosting the rentals up so high that it now seems I will be unable to make any money as long as the present contracts are in force.

It naturally goes without saying that I have got to have reductions all along the line from five exchanges. I am writing four other exchange head offices today.

Yours very truly,

D.A. Boyle[2]

Some two weeks later, Boyle had his response from MGM Canada. Mr. Gould explains, in a letter dated March 24, his records show the Empress ordered just three MGM pictures, all of them in 1950, and suggests Boyle's 1949 financial situation was based on films from other distributors. However, Gould notes:

I want you to know, Mr. Boyle, we are seriously interested in the operation of the theatres in small towns. We want to see them all make money. We do not expect to get rentals that we are not entitled to. Therefore, as far as we are concerned, I suggest that you see how our pictures do for you during the next three or four months. After that, it will be time for us to discuss whether or not you are entitled to reductions.

You must remember that during all the good years, Mr. Boyle, during the war years when business was very good, we were only getting a top rental of $50., and I am sure our pictures must have been very, very profitable to you. However, we will not discuss that further, and look at the performance of our pictures from now on. I am sure, in taking the above view, we are being very fair, and I want to point out to you, Mr. Boyle, that where we split at $260., as we do with the top pictures in your theatre, actually we are only getting 25%, which we feel is very reasonable.[3]

Boyle's letter also reached Skorey's desk at Fox in Calgary, who mildly chided the Empress manager's explanation that Macleod presented a limited amount of business for the theatre. Skorey notes in his March 16 reply to Boyle that he had recently attended an exhibitors' seminar, presumably in the United States, at which he learned:

...there is more money standing in the banks today than ever before (and I believe this is also applicable to Canada) and in view of the fact that less than 15% of the people are now regular show-goers, there is certainly a vast room for improvement in attendance. There are many people that haven't been attending shows that must be encouraged to attend if this industry is to survive.[4]

When he wasn't drafting letters to distributors, taking tickets, building elaborate promotional pieces and serving as the face of the Empress, Dan Boyle filled another necessary role at the Empress: bouncer. As he explained the scrapes on his face to his daughter one morning at breakfast, the night previous a rowdy patron had picked a fight when asked to leave. As Dan engaged the miscreant, his wife Edna called the police and helped her husband send the troublemaker on his way by adding a few choice words of her own, delivered, as she was later to boast, with perfect grammar and free of swearing. Edna also displayed her aplomb when, one evening, an anonymous caller told her a bomb had been planted in the Empress. Refusing to be rattled, Edna told the caller not to be so silly and hung up. As she recounted the incident to Dan at evening's end, Edna explained her hesitance in informing him of the call, saying she thought he might feel compelled to give patrons their money back and, after all, the night's crowd had been such a good one.[5]

As a child of a theatre owner, Mary Yvonne had special access – a backstage pass of sorts – to the nooks and corners of the Empress. Steep, rickety stairs took her into the basement, an exotic place where she could watch her father create doll houses and Ferris wheels for her, and where she could read, and wonder at, graffiti left by Empress performers: the LaBelle Dancing Twins; Texas Tommy and his Wonder Horse Baby Doll/ Purple Sage Riders - Aug. 5, 1935/address/Isabella/Box 45/Calif.; Wilfred Percy Pearson Comic Opera; and 'Ask Omar - Mentalist and Magician. For Omar, Dan had to install special wiring to enable the magician to eavesdrop on conversations and come up with "amazing" pieces of information about the audience.

Boyle's close affiliation with the Commonwealth Air Training Plan, and his support for the war effort, created friendships with several base commanders, some of whom kept up relations upon their return to Britain. In August 1943, Wing Commander M. Brown wrote to Boyle from overseas to thank the people of Macleod for their hospitality:

> At last I have arrived in the wee country and now that I am settled, I feel that I should try in some manner to let you know how much the Browns enjoyed living in your community. I wish you would pass the word on to the members of the Board of Trade and thank them for their fine co-operation during my office as Commanding Officer, and to thank them also for their kind hospitality. Macleod and its people are indeed emblematic of the finest traditions of the West and I want you to know that Mrs. Brown and I will always think of our residence in your community as the most pleasant period of our service life.[6]

Brown's letter goes on to cast aspersions on the poker-playing acumen of southern Alberta farmers, to whom, it's suspected, he lost frequently. He suggests a rematch on his home turf based on "pounds, shillings and pence." He also praised Boyle for allowing the air force band, Slipstream, to mount periodic Sunday evening performances in the Empress free of charge.

The Empress was, like any other business, at the mercy of Calgary Power. Outages during the 1940s and '50s, seemed to happen with some frequency due to heavy snow, lightning or other misfortune. These power failures were a source of consternation to Boyle, who maintained a strict policy of "the show must go on." Packed houses indicated their displeasure by booing and stamping of feet; money was often refunded. On one occasion, the film scheduled for the following two nights didn't arrive on the Greyhound from Calgary. In a feat of aeronautic flair, Boyle's nephew, Howard Sandgathe, a pilot in Calgary, flew the missing reels to Macleod, thus saving the day and making headlines in the *Macleod Gazette*. Sandgathe later became one of the first pilots for Trans Canada Airlines (now Air Canada).[7]

Power failures and missing films weren't enough to shut down the Empress; fire, however, was. In January of 1942, the Boyles were alerted by phone that fire had broken out in the theatre, caused by a blowtorch explosion. Norman McDonald,

AS A CHILD OF A THEATRE OWNER, MARY YVONNE HAD SPECIAL ACCESS – A BACKSTAGE PASS OF SORTS – TO THE NOOKS AND CORNERS OF THE EMPRESS.

the Empress's projectionist, had been doing some light soldering in the rewind room at 6 p.m., an hour before curtain time, when his torch began to flame. He rushed to get an extinguisher but, before he could reach one, an explosion ripped off plaster, knocked McDonald through the projection room and out a spring door onto the stairway. Minutes later, the projection and rewind room were enveloped in flames. When the Macleod fire brigade responded, the fire appeared to have the upper hand, but was soon under control. It had, however, badly damaged the Empress's projection room and destroyed about $2,000 worth of films.

When Boyle and brigade chief Bud Day inspected the building, they discovered the safety shutters between the projection room and the auditorium had functioned perfectly, dropping into position at the fire's outbreak and saving the rest of the building. As for poor McDonald, he was uninjured but for singed hair; shaken, he still managed to help clean up in the aftermath.[8]

Mary Yvonne and her brother Neil, along with the Hart boys, served as ushers at one time or another, the Harts in their red Macleod Imperials orchestra jackets. During her Grade 9 year, Mary Yvonne earned $1 on Saturday nights by patrolling balcony seating, alerting the ticket booth as seats were filled to avoid overselling. It was an easy job, with far less inherent excitement than Neil encountered on the lower level, especially during raucous Saturday matinees. These were occasions where children counting on obscurity in the darkened auditorium, indulged in shenanigans, from throwing wads of gum and stones at the screen, dropping Popsicles down the necks of rivals, squirting the unsuspecting with water pistols, to the more serious mischief of fisticuffs and vandalism to Empress upholstery.

Ushers were often required to extricate small feet lodged in theatre seats, drinks were frequently spilled, and young patrons were often found cowering in the lobby during particularly frightening features, often in need of a reassuring hand-holding,

> IF ANY OTHER BOYLE LEFT A
> LASTING MARK ON THE EMPRESS,
> IT WAS DAN AND EDNA'S SON,
> THE ARTIST NEIL BOYLE.

while, back on screen, a mummy, vampire or werewolf eviscerated another victim. Yes, matinees were the trenches of the theatre business; timidity was quickly exposed, the weak became prey for the mob and promising show business careers were swept down the aisle like so many discarded popcorn boxes.

Edna Boyle, wife, mother, maven of the ticket booth, creator of Snow White costumes, had already sewn one set of Empress curtains when CinemaScope challenged her once again. The wider screen needed far larger drapes, and Edna produced them from her living and dining rooms, running the rich, red fabric through her portable Singer sewing machine.

Dan, too, had his challenges. A theatre-owner in a one-cinema town, much like his patrons, is a bit of a captive audience. Movie fans could be difficult to please, each one with a favourite genre or particular dislike for another and all knew where Dan Boyle lived, so to speak. If he had a safety zone, it was during the Fort Macleod Stampede, when any western would ensure crowd contentment, ready as they were for cowboy action.

By the time of his sudden death at 69 from heart failure in 1963, Dan Boyle had managed eight Victory Loan campaigns during the Second World War, served on town council, become an honorary chief of both the Peigan and Blood bands, been a driving force in the development of the town's annual stampede and the construction of its replica fort, been named the community's citizen of the year for 1960, hobnobbed with movie stars in Hollywood.[9] Perhaps most significantly, Boyle left the Empress in its 51st year in far better standing than he found it almost three decades earlier. The year Boyle passed away, Edna sold the theatre to Richard Vincent Kiefer who, a decade later, sold it to Gerardus Antonius Goedhart. Following the sale to Keifer, Edna moved to Vancouver to be closer to her daughter Mary Yvonne Dunne. Edna died at 79 on February 16, 1983 and was buried beside her beloved Dan in the cemetery in Fort Macleod.

Hand painted sign showing premium prices for seating in the balcony is part of a collection of artifacts held by the Empress Theatre.

If any other Boyle left a lasting mark on the Empress, it was Dan and Edna's son, the artist Neil Boyle. Theatre patrons waiting for performances to begin have long been treated to Neil's grand paintings, installed on the theatre's walls in 2005 under the Alberta Centennial Legacy Program. Incorporating the artwork of a true son of southern Alberta, regardless of how far he had roamed or how successful he had become, seemed fitting to the theatre's board of directors.

Here, then, on the Empress walls ensconced in the false windows once covered in wallpaper are Neil Boyle's tributes to Bull's Head, Red Crow, Crowfoot, James Macleod, Dan Boyle, Faye Wray, W.C. Fields and Bronco Billy Anderson.

Neil Boyle had breathed in as much Empress dust as anyone in town. A boy whose father owns the place is fated to spend considerable time within its varied spaces. Neil took his place in the seats watching every movie through the 1930s and '40s (his favourite: a Jack Benny film, *The Horn Blows at Midnight*), trod the stage as an amateur thespian, and patrolled the aisles as an usher.

An early addiction to art set Neil on his career path, first as an illustrator and then as a fine artist and teacher. Encouraged in his endeavours by his parents, Boyle finished high school and began his formal artistic education at the Banff School of Fine Arts. Later, he studied at the Chouinard Art Institute and Art Center College of Design in Los Angeles, where many of Walt Disney's artists were discovered. This connection may have led to the mistaken belief that Boyle worked for Disney. Rather, Boyle taught at art schools in Los Angeles and held an associate professorship with the University of California at Long Beach and Northridge. He taught for 15 years at the California Art Institute in Westlake Village.[10] Many of his works have illustrated major publications such as *Reader's Digest* and *Cosmopolitan*.[11]

A chat with Neil's contemporaries, brothers Bob and Ken Hart, provides a more animated portrait of the man. Bob Hart, a life-long citizen of Fort Macleod, recalls Neil Boyle as a one-of-the-guys types who did well in school and had a little acting talent for those moments when it came in handy. Hart remembers Dan Boyle, father and theatre-owner, as a generous man who would give the Empress freely to the high school band, which put on performances there to raise money for instruments. "He'd just give us the theatre," says Hart. "We'd put on acts for the community. Dan even helped build props in the basement."

Bob Hart remembers the opening of the new balcony, built to accommodate the increased business from the air base, recalling how he and his friends lined up to get seats upstairs. Later Bob played trumpet and drums in a group called the Imperials, so named as they were in part sponsored by the Imperial Oil station in town. The two Harts earned money as kids, to pay the 15-cent Empress admission and for traditional childhood sundries, through deliveries: Ken was into groceries, while Bob distributed icebox ice and meat. A typical Saturday night outside the Empress was a blur of horse-drawn wagons and farm trucks fuelled with 11-cents-a-gallon gasoline. Ken's flair for acting – he's been the town crier for every Fort Macleod Santa Clause Parade – earned him spots in two of the films shot in town: the period drama *Passchendaele* in 2008, and *Brokeback Mountain* in 2005. Both movies, naturally, were hits at the Empress.[12]

> AS NEIL MADE HIS WAY DOWN THE FAMILIAR AISLE, TOWNSPEOPLE AND PATRONS, THEATRE STAFF AND DIRECTORS GREETED HIM WITH A STANDING OVATION

Besides the reminiscence of his boyhood pals, the Internet also adds texture to the life and times of Neil Boyle. A website for enthusiasts of art from the 1940s and '50s, contains these anonymous comments from his fans:

> He was the one of the greatest characters I ever met, and one of the most fearless painters – and teachers – I ever saw...alternating fantastic insights into drawing and painting with hysterical anecdotes from his career the whole time. It was fantastic. There is a terrific series of videos on YouTube of another demonstration by Neil, including his pithy comments on both illustration and fine art from a man who had long and successful careers at both.
>
> There's a huge collection of Neil's paintings at Molly Malone's Pub on 6th and Fairfax here in Los Angeles. It's worth a visit.[13]

In the noted video, Boyle continuously jokes with his audience, referring to himself as a "recovering illustrator" and boasting that his art is "completely washable." One fan quotes him as saying, "The difference between illustration and fine art is a frame."

Boyle was honoured for his commercial work by the Society of Illustrators in New York, Los Angeles, and the Los Angeles Art Directors Club. He joined just six living recipients of a Lifetime Achievement Award from the Society of Illustrators in Los Angeles. Four of his works graced the commemorative U.S. Bicentennial stamp series "Contributors to the Cause." More than 40 of his works were chosen for the U.S. Air Force Art Collection in the Smithsonian, the Pentagon and in their traveling shows. His work hangs at NASA's Kennedy Space Center.

Before he had legitimate letters after his name, Boyle, with self-deprecating humor, added BSWCA to his signatures, the letters standing for Big Shot West Coast Artist. Boyle, however, was never too much of a "big shot" to forget his southern Alberta roots. When his art was celebrated at the Empress in late 2005, less than two months before his death at 74 from throat cancer on February 4, 2006, Boyle returned for the event, a day captured by Fort Macleod writer Bonnie Kennedy: "As Neil made his way down the familiar aisle, townspeople and patrons, theatre staff and directors greeted him with a standing ovation claiming as their own both the man and his eloquent tribute to the past."[14]

Betty Boyle, Neil's second wife, says her late husband chose to depict characters such as Wray and Fields because they were among his favourites. Painting in the basement of his house in Cumberland on Vancouver Island, and constricted by the eight-foot ceiling, Boyle fixed to the wall as many feet of canvas as he could, stood on the rest, and scrolled up the canvas as he painted. Betty, an accomplished artist in her own right who met Neil while taking one of his courses, explains the work was created in the illustration style; the works are not "filled in" to the frames, but rather use white space for their backgrounds. The paintings, she says in the vernacular of the illustrator, "communicate well" with the viewer. Neil took a year to finish the six works, which he did the summer before he died.[15]

ON AN EVENING in late 1977, Darrel Fraser prepared to perform for a packed house at the Empress Theatre. The overflow crowd filling the 300-plus seats had been anticipating this night for some time, and Fraser knew only his best would be good enough to send folks home with the memories they'd come expecting to make. His skills, honed during many previous shows, were at their peak, but he understood past performances counted for nothing on this night of nights. One wrong move, one small slip, and the excitement would drain from the building like champagne down a gutter. He arrived early, ran through his routine, careful not to rush it, and, as curtain time approached, sensed that delicious nervousness known only to those in the theatre business. The crowd, boisterous for the past half hour, quieted as the house lights dimmed. Just as the curtains began to part, Fraser steadied his nerves and allowed tradition and a practiced regimen of timing and co-ordination to take over. He held his breath, flipped a switch and, to perfection, the opening frames of *Star Wars* flooded from his projection booth onto the Empress screen. Darrel Fraser, Class I Alberta projectionist, had flawlessly recreated a galaxy far, far away for an awestruck audience.

It was, says Fraser, the most memorable evening in his 15 years on the job and due to the movie's incredible hype, the only time in his career he witnessed a standing-room-only house for a film. Born and raised in southern Alberta, Fraser, like Mary Yvonne Boyle, saw *Snow White and the Seven Dwarfs* at the Empress and recalls Mary Yvonne's father Dan giving away movie posters to children. The Fraser family's connection to the theatre is long-standing; Blanche Fraser, Darrel's grandmother, was one of the first pianists in 1912. After operating a mixed farm just south of town most of his life, he was lured into the projectionist business by a friend who was similarly employed. He attained his Alberta third-class projectionist's certificate in 1976 after easily earning a pass on the required exam and sending in his $10. Through the next few months, Fraser scored his second- and first-class tickets.

Today's modern equipment has removed much of the excitement from the projectionist's art, such as the adrenalin rush derived from working with highly flammable silver nitrate film and carbon-arc bulbs. The combustible combination, set in a tiny enclave in the rear of a darkened theatre crowded with humanity, made for interesting times for projectionists, knowing that one wrong move could wipe out a fair-sized chunk of the town's population even on a slow night. The obvious hazards dictated that projectionists acquire safety certification. When silver nitrate was ultimately replaced by technological advances in film production, the danger of immolating friends and neighbours during their night at the movies was greatly lessened.

As Empress projectionist, Fraser picked up movies from the Greyhound depot and rewound them onto the better show reels from cheaper shipping reels. Two projectors

CHAPTER NINE

# THE PHANTOM OF THE OPERA HOUSE

were required, each able to hold about 20 minutes of film. Cue marks were printed on each reel of film to indicate when a projector switch was approaching, and a bell also sounded in case the projectionist had fallen asleep during drearier offerings. Once the first switch was made, Fraser would rewind the reel, remove it from the projector, and install the third reel. During the screening of a 90-minute movie, the projectionist switched between machines up to five times.

Although carbon arc lights provided excellent illumination for movies, they were dirty and required considerable maintenance. The light was produced by an arc of electricity between two carbon rods. The process required daily maintenance; Fraser cleaned and lubricated the projectors every night. Later, that arc was produced by xenon in a sealed glass unit. Xenon produced a sunlight spectrum for more natural colours. One drawback: they explode if touched by fingertips. Yes, the craft of the movie projectionist in the non-digital age required much more than an ability to hit the on switch. Besides the technical expertise required, Fraser had to keep his head in the game; he admits occasions arose where mistakes were made. Reels were sometimes shown out of order, or incorrectly rewound so that the soundtrack, located along one edge of the film, ended up on the wrong side returning the Empress to a silent-movie house. Fraser took solace at those moments by recalling what his mentor, Jim McKenna, had once told him: it doesn't matter in what order the reels are shown as long as the first one is first, the last is last, and you show them all.

For all those 15 years of nights in the projection room, Fraser worked with the smell of fresh popcorn wafting upwards from the concession booth directly below, skewering any determination he might have rallied to cut out junk food. While Darrel tended the projectors upstairs, his wife Flory worked directly below him selling treats. One memorable night, Fraser put his foot through the projection room's crawl space floor, sending half a century of accumulated dirt into the concession area. He "went on strike" one Sunday evening after a showing of *The Texas Chainsaw Massacre*, a movie that so offended Fraser he refused to show it

twice. And it was from his projection booth Fraser determined he needed glasses after being informed by patrons the movie being shown was out of focus. Still, Fraser describes his years in the booth as a labour of love, both of the craft and of the movies; getting paid to watch was a bonus, even if catching the entire film, with all his jumping between reels, required viewing each one three times.[1]

Fraser was Empress projectionist during the five years the theatre was owned by Larry and Edith Becker. For the Beckers, Darrel Fraser was "the theatre's angel" who could fix anything that needed it and, with his wife and sons, was as much a part of the Empress family as were the Beckers. They had purchased the business in September 1977 from Gerardus Antonius Goedhart after buying the theatre in Waterton the year before. The Beckers added the operation in Pincher Creek in 1979, creating a profitable three-community movie circuit. They ensured the Empress was the first small-town theatre in the area to show *Star Wars*, which highlighted their grand opening. The Beckers ran two showings a night, brought in Saturday matinees geared to children, and offered a lone Sunday-evening "special" film. The Beckers operated the Empress for a little more than 20 hours a week, offering the rest of the time to the community at no charge other than expenses.

Now divorced, the Beckers are still in show biz. Larry operates the Waterton theatre, while Edith leases her ownership of the Pincher Creek theatre and operates an arts shop in Waterton. She spends her weekdays in Calgary as a movie booking agent; one of her clients is the Empress Theatre, for which she retains a deep affection. Billing herself as the "world's oldest candy girl," she worked the Empress concession booth, while her two-month-old son Travis slept nearby, unaware of the hubbub around him. It wasn't far from her own upbringing: she "grew up" in the theatre in Elk Point, Alberta, owned at the time by her parents. As a teen she worked for Famous Players as a "candy girl" and, to little surprise, she met Larry as the two worked at the Palace Theatre in Calgary. In 1979, during the filming of *Wild Horse Hank*, starring Linda Blair (*The Exorcist*), in Waterton Lakes

National Park, the Beckers allowed the production company to screen its "dailies" in the theatre, an opportunity that drew Larry into film production; he served as a director of the Alberta Motion Picture Theatre Association and as an assistant editor on other made-in-Alberta films such as Clint Eastwood's *Unforgiven* and *Cool Runnings* with John Candy, the story of the Jamaican bobsleigh team at the Calgary Olympics.

During one stretch of their ownership, the Beckers showed "special" films on Sunday nights. The RCMP, says Edith, would show up at the scheduled start time and go straight to the projection booth to view the movies. During one of her horror-series offerings, Edith recalls that in the middle of a particularly suspenseful scene a resident cat rubbed up against the leg of a female patron. If yawns are contagious, so too are screams, and hers sent the entire theatre into a frenzy.[2]

After moving to Pincher Creek in 1979, Larry Becker advertised the Empress for sale. In his newspaper advertisement, Becker noted the Empress had realized sales of $78,000 in 1978, returning a profit of more than $24,000 after depreciation and income tax. His asking price was $135,000.[3]

Just before the Beckers finally sold the Empress in 1982, Edith had hoped to bring local drama productions to the theatre's stage. Since forming in 1979, the Fort Macleod Dramatic Society had been performing in school gymnasiums, while the Empress with its perfect acoustics, dynamic stage and lighting and proper seating served the community as little more than a movie house for some three decades. The society had already mounted several worthy productions when, in 1982, it brought Agatha Christie's *The Mousetrap* to the Empress. *The Mousetrap* was the troupe's second Christie play after staging *Murder at the Vicarage*. Sebastian David, a key player in the society, recalls few in Fort Macleod had ever seen a stage play prior to the production of *Murder*. *Mousetrap* received considerable local press and notoriety, in part, because it returned live theatre to the Empress. The production, which ran three nights, was well received by the community and, recalls David, made enough money to purchase a spotlight still in use at the Empress.

During its run the society staged comedies, musicals and dramas (from *Barefoot in the Park* to *Anne of Green Gables*). While actors, says David, were relatively easy to find, personnel for production roles were difficult to locate. Eventually, the Fort Macleod Dramatic Society ran out of steam and ceased productions in 1993.

As the 1980s drew down, another champion of live theatre arose. Fort Macleod and District Allied Arts, under the leadership of Marj Hatton, presented a fall and winter concert series, beginning in 1988-'89. Once Allied Arts, with the assistance of the theatre manager and staff, had booked performers for a four-concert series, tickets were printed and Hatton and a crew of volunteers canvassed every household in Fort Macleod to ensure the series' success. The canvassers, says Delle Schmidt, were welcomed at the door and even householders who didn't buy series tickets often gave donations to the theatre.[4]

After the initial series, Allied Arts realized the theatre required a piano and staged a benefit concert to raise the money. With wholehearted community support, a grand piano was installed at the theatre in 1992; it is still in use today. Allied Arts continued as presenter of the concert series until the mid 1990s when the series was turned over to the Empress Theatre Society.

One highly documented feature of the theatre – an element far less corporeal than the bricks, the management or the programming – is the Empress ghost. The phantom of the opera house, so to speak, has been haunting the theatre for several years. Phenomena such as lights flicking on, an unexplained noise over the intercom, a door suddenly slammed shut, a lost earring magically discovered in a high-traffic hallway days after the area had been carefully searched were common. The spritely presence has been experienced in diverse ways by several people, particularly by staff members and others working in the theatre for extended periods of time. The experiences are varied and people's reactions to them are wide-ranging.

Former owner Edith Becker admits to being badly frightened one morning. While she was walking down the right aisle toward the stage, a seat slowly lowered into position, stopping her in her tracks. It was evident, says Becker, that she was in the presence of something remarkable enough to make whatever she had been heading to the stage for seem no longer important.[5]

Some who have encountered the phantom believe it to be the restless spirit of long-time owner Dan Boyle, while others refer to it simply as "Ed," once a theatre maintenance man. Gerard Gibbs, a former Empress manager now living in the United States, supports the idea that Dan might be the resident ghost. Gibbs understood that the mysticism apparently started in the 1980s during the Great West Theatre years. During rehearsals, which often took place at odd hours, lights would inexplicably flicker and bizarre noises could be heard by cast and crew.

Although Gibbs never actually saw the ghost during his tenure, he was nonetheless spooked. After hearing enough stories of others who had experienced the phantom, he allowed a ghost-hunting group from Calgary to use a light-sensitive surveillance system in the darkened theatre. The equipment picked up floating white shadows; the play-back frightened Gibbs so badly, he turned it off, declaring later, "It was too much for me."[6]

Theatre employee, Sharon Hellman, is a believer whose first memories of the ghost go back to girlhood days. A regular attendee at matinees, she would sashay, as she describes, through the lobby like a princess entering a castle waiting for the day she would be allowed to watch a movie from the balcony – seating that was, at that time, reserved for teens and adults. It was an apparition in the main theatre – a woman dressed in a beautiful white gown walking down the west aisle – she recalls most vividly. As the spectre approached the stage, it faded from view. Hellman's sightings have not been restricted to females, however. She also saw a male figure – most believe the ghost to be male – in a mirror in an old Empress bathroom.[7]

Ryland Moranz, Empress sound technician, has long suspected the ghost to be a regular visitor to the balcony. After ensuring all the seats are in the upright position following performances, he's found the same one placed down, as if someone had been sitting in it. The seat is in proper repair; there is no apparent reason for it to drop unaided.[8]

Still others describe a feeling of being watched: Neil Plourde, a carpenter who worked on the theatre restoration project in the 1980s, felt as if several "somethings" watched him whenever he worked in the theatre alone. Former employee Wendy Rigaux experienced the sensation she was never alone when she worked in the rear of the basement. While it has been suggested that anyone aware that the Empress is haunted might be more likely to conjure all manner of weirdness, it seems that even those who were completely unaware have experienced a presence. Sarah McLachlan's band had never heard of the Empress ghost before appearing in February 1992; still, band members had an odd sensation that something was watching them as they walked up the backstage stairs.[9]

Jim Layton, a former Empress employee, was so thoroughly spooked on two consecutive nights, he resigned rather than work alone in what he considered haunted surroundings. The first night, after locking himself in the theatre, he heard footsteps upstairs while he waxed the floor in the green room. The next evening, as he waited in the lobby for the floor to dry, he heard a noise like wind inside the theatre on what was a calm night outside.

Juran Greene, another former manager, claims he never actually saw the ghost, though he doesn't deny that he experienced its presence on several occasions. Finding lights burning after he had shut them off, he at first assumed the phenomenon was nothing more than a prank being pulled at his expense. His explanation, however, fell short that night. While working late in his basement office, Greene, too, heard footsteps above him. After a close inspection of the building, he returned to his office, only to again hear the footsteps; a second reconnaissance failed to explain the footfalls Greene was certain he had not imagined.

Settling his prodigious frame into one of the theatre's double seats, Greene waited in the darkened theatre for whomever or whatever was walking the aisle. Moments later, he says, he felt a presence and, being the feisty person he is, Greene challenged it by declaring in a loud voice that he would not be frightened off the premises by ectoplasm. His rant was barely finished when the ensuing silence was shattered by a ladder tipping and falling to the theatre floor. Unsure which way to go, Greene walked to the back of theatre and added, "I mean it; I'm not leaving."[10]

Greene also recalls that following an encounter with the spirit, a violinist in a group had to be talked back into the Empress for a night's performance. After placing their equipment in the theatre, the band headed out to a pre-show dinner when the violinist ran back to retrieve his wallet from an unlocked dressing room. Finding himself trapped inside when the door closed and would not open, the musician panicked exclaiming, "Oh god, please let me out!" – charmed words, apparently, as the door suddenly swung open.[11]

Daniel Boyle ...
Chief Bullhorn

**Neil Boyle painting of his father, Daniel Boyle, who owned the Empress for a quarter of its existence.**

**Neil Boyle painting of American comedian W. C. Fields.**

**Images Courtesy: Betty Boyle**

A BIT OF A SEDUCTRESS, the Empress has enchanted many of those who have worked with her during her first ten decades, flirting just enough to get what she needs before moving on to the next suitor. One who fell hard and fast for her charms was Jim Mountain. He became smitten during his work compiling an inventory of historical structures from Nanton south for Alberta Culture and Historic Sites from 1977 to 1979. Mountain found the Empress during his review of downtown Fort Macleod and immediately recognized the lady she was. Elsewhere across the province, buildings still standing from the early 1900s had either been demolished or so altered as to be rendered unremarkable historically. But here, Mountain discovered time had done little to alter the Empress's appearance from her original 1912 appearance.

As the town's website explains:

> During the winter of 1980-81 Gateway Consultants of Calgary conducted a study of the old commercial core. They produced a working concept document which addressed the issue of designating that portion of the downtown as a Provincial Historic Area under the Alberta Historical Resources Act. A committee was formed comprised of representatives of the Municipal and Provincial Governments, the town business community, the regional planning commission and the Alberta Historical Resources Foundation. Their mandate was to examine ways and means of revising and implementing the Historic Area concept plan. A series of public meetings was conducted during the autumn and winter of 1981-82 and ultimately in March '82, the town council moved that the plan be adopted and submitted to the Alberta Legislature as an Order-in-Council. The plan was ratified, a Historic Area created, design guidelines implemented for buildings within the area, and a revolving fund set up to provide seed money for building revitalization. The Heritage Canada Main Street Program then provided their experience from other Canadian communities in working with small town revitalization.[1]

Working from an office in Lethbridge, Mountain held a series of meetings at the Java Shop, a popular locale in Fort Macleod, listening and taking voluminous notes as townsfolk spoke from the heart about what they envisioned for the few blocks of history along Main Street. The more he listened, the more he recognized Fort Macleod's potential to become a demonstration model for the Heritage Canada Main Street program which was, at the time, searching for a suitable candidate.[2]

Fort Macleod was not the province's first choice to be the initial heritage showpiece. It had originally chosen Coleman, one of the five communities of the Crowsnest Pass. But people there were not keen to be involved in the scheme. The atmosphere was different in Fort Macleod, and the community spirit generated for the project led to the town's selection for the honour.

CHAPTER TEN

# THAT BUILDING WON'T EVER LET THEM DOWN

Photo: Sharon Monical

1986 Great West Theatre Production *Shake, Rattle and Roll*.
Cast:   Rear, left to right – Candice Elzinga, Jaybo Russell, Keith O'Sullivan,
Kelly Roberts, Narda McCarroll
Front, left to right – David Loney, Marselle Jobs, Greg Jarvie,
Lynne Richardson, Jeff Carlson.

Mountain's application to the federal program was accepted and, after winning hearts and minds in the town with his vision and enthusiasm, he was offered the chance to guide the project as its co-ordinator. Those who worked closest with him in the Fort Macleod Provincial Area History Society Main Street Project office, Louise Heric and Sharon Monical, consider Mountain a visionary some 30 years later.[3] He started the famed Fort Macleod Santa Claus Parade, still an annual event in the community, and he dedicated himself to returning the Empress to its position as the town's cultural centre.

In August 1982, the Main Street project, worth more than $1 million, began with Mountain taking stock of the town's assets and determining how to turn them into a positive social, cultural and economic benefit to the community. Mountain admits the one property he considered the star attraction was the Empress, a theatre – an entertainment venue – located directly on the main drag. The owner of the day, Suresh Prasad, had purchased the Empress the year previous from Larry Becker. Under Prasad, the Empress operated as the town's lone movie theatre, with films projected on a screen tacked to the front of the stage. With no basement at the time, the stage had become a storage area, littered with junk.

In 1983, Prasad gave use of the Empress to the newly formed Great West Summer Theatre Company during the day, retaining the evenings for movies. That schedule meant Great West had to put on two shows a day, in the morning and afternoon, not exactly prime time for theatre. Nonetheless, the plays went ahead, two a summer, with Prasad taking half the gate. At first, those behind the project believed melodrama would be the best format to draw crowds, recall Heric and Monical. Mountain's wife, Kaija, was at the time a drama student at the University of Lethbridge. She convinced one of her professors, Brian Parkinson, to mentor the 10 young actors in the company, everyone being paid through a student summer employment grant. The troupe wrote its own material, much based on the area's history, and borrowed costumes and props from the community. With funding from Alberta Culture, Parkinson and his players staged *Egad What a Cad* and *Dastardly Deed at the Grill*, charging a top price of $1. Turnouts were meager, however, drawing an average of 15 a performance, while a decent Friday night might bring in 40.[4]

Audiences were small despite Mountain's heroic attempts to attract interest. He often ambushed tour buses that stopped at the nearby Fort Museum. One such hijacking involved a busload of Americans from Phoenix on its way to Banff and almost caused a fight between passengers eager to see the 10 a.m. show and a driver bent on meeting his appointed schedule. Another target was a group of boy scouts. Mountain would take along the actors, dressed in costume, on these forays to heighten enthusiasm.

Director Parkinson kept at it; Great West employed melodrama for two more years, then slowly added music and blurred historical accuracy to create a more vibrant product. In 1985, *Puttin' on the Glitz* brought in 160 people a night.[5] The melodramas were successful enough but no one involved was prepared for the enthusiastic public response to the presentation of musicals. The first, *Shake, Rattle and Roll* in 1986, attracted capacity crowds from throughout the region. People lined Main Street for a chance to see the show; some nights, up to 200 were turned away thanks to another sold-out performance. As word spread of the show's popularity and the scarcity of seating, crowds began lining up at 6:30 p.m. for an 8 p.m. start. The 400 or so lucky enough to get in were treated to high-energy performances by a cast of young folk who could sing, dance, deliver one-liners and, after all that, greet patrons on the street following each performance; the joint was jumping again. That year, *Shake* drew 10,000 people to the Empress, vetting the company's credentials – and filling the Empress – for the next three years.[6]

Recall, these shows were put on prior to the renovations that would add a basement to the Empress. The ticket booth, concession area and bathrooms were all crammed together just inside the doors. If organizers once fretted about empty seats, they now feared safety inspections from overcrowding. For many southern Albertans, summer never felt quite complete without a trip to Fort Macleod and the antics at the Empress. This vital new role for the Empress ended following the 1989 show when, due to politics and economics, the troupe moved to Lethbridge and reformed as New West Theatre; its sold-out summer shows continue to this day.

By 1988, money secured for the Main Street project was put into upgrading the Empress, the second structure to be restored after Hodnutt's Pharmacy. The theatre was now owned by the town, purchased from Prasad for some $110,000. Wes Olmstead, Fort Macleod's then-mayor, terms the purchase, subsequent renovations and continued operation by the town as a true community effort. "A lot of private money was going into the restoration of private buildings on Main Street," says Olmstead. "We felt some of it could be used to restore a public building. The community agreed and supported our initiative. I think with time we all realize what a legacy we created."[7]

Of the $600,000 for theatre restoration, some was spent on cosmetics and some on foundational work, such as the excavation of a full basement. Because of its provincial heritage designation, the Empress had to be handled with extreme care, the job of a design and review committee. Clearly, someone was needed who could direct traffic, who could ensure the Empress kept her shoulders square to the street while having her bottom renovated. Jim Mountain was able to find the right person, an architecture intern named Art Ferrari who was looking for hands-on experience to attain his professional designation while working with Bradley T. Goss, Architect. Ferrari, who died suddenly in July 2011, brought an aura of flamboyance to the Main Street Office, what with his exotic surname and a penchant for peppering his comments with references to Milan, Italy.

The project afforded Ferrari little room for maneuvering, literally. The Empress was, as it is today, hemmed in on both sides. The downstairs consisted of tiny dressing rooms, an existing green room, an ancient furnace room and dirt floors. The only way to expand was below ground. The excavation of a basement below a building in its seventies, therefore, was a bit like playing a game of Jenga: one wrong move and a major piece of community history comes crashing down upsetting the neighbours on both sides. To avoid such a faux pas, Ferrari employed an abundance of underpinning, reinforcing the Empress as the dirt was removed beneath her.

As the project crept on, Ferrari's trepidations grew. He understood the importance of the project to the entire town, and likely thought of the alternative: construction of a separate building in the parking lot. The task of renovation required an incredible amount of manual labour and hands-on know-how. For both, Ferrari turned to Al Park, a veteran Fort Macleod excavator who knows as much about the first 20 feet of ground below the town as anyone alive. Park closed the alley, removed the rear foundation and set up heaters to thaw the February frost. It took most of a week to warm the ground down the requisite 12 feet to allow work to begin. Digging by hand down the middle of the building until they had room to use a Bobcat, Park's crew tunneled 90 degrees from the spine every four feet to build a foundation using concrete and steel posts. At one point, workers discovered sand in the existing side foundation, not a good sign for a weight-bearing wall, and Ferrari had nightmares of the adjacent business crumbling into the Empress basement. Park managed to patch a small cave-in and secure the section with a double wall. Theatre patrons heading to the green room for intermission refreshments are likely unaware the sight of the mishap is now a wall five feet thick, located a step or two along the hallway from the bottom of the stairs. It's all stable now but, for a few moments in 1988, Park was convinced he was looking up at the floor of the neighbouring drycleaners (now home to the Fort Macleod Senior Citizens' Association).

The excavation – really a mining operation under a 76-year-old building sitting on gravel with a two-foot crawl space – also turned up a few mementoes of a time when the lot stood empty and might have been used as an impromptu dumping ground. Park found women's high-top leather shoes, liquor bottles and more in several piles as he worked. He believes the shoes predated 1900.

Park and his crew built a ramp from the alley into the raw basement to remove dirt and gravel, and to run concrete in by wheelbarrow. They also created a tunnel north under the alley, which today provides a walkway from the basement of the Empress to a seemingly remote storage facility standing in the parking lot.[8]

Once the heavy lifting was complete underneath the Empress, Ferrari moved in and up. Taking the requisite care to remain true to the Empress's history, he brought the building in line with the Alberta Building Code. Safety rails were added to the balcony. Carpets and linoleum were matched as closely as possible; carpet and fabric to re-upholster the seats were imported from the southern United States. No debate was allowed on the seating colour: it had always been red; no other colour would do. (When the seats were removed for re-upholstering, the Empress made use of the down time to throw a *Rocky Horror Picture Show* event.) The carpet, from a mill in Atlanta, was chosen for its high wear and fire retardant features. The curtain colour was based on the best research available, a dark crimson. The front brickwork was all repointed, and the marquee restored. In all,

the work lasted nine months and, Ferrari recalls, was an exciting time of learning for all involved.

Ferrari believed Western Canada was a relatively young part of the country, with little historical architecture of note; those who rip down buildings rather than restoring them make decisions that keep the country from securing a history. Months after the work was completed, while in line for a performance at the Empress, Ferrari at last understood the full significance of the theatre restoration. It remained a source of pride for him, though he later designed buildings of a much greater size and scope. Shortly before his death Ferrari, by then a respected partner of Ferrari Westwood Babits Architects in Lethbridge, explained that if he were to head a restoration project on the Empress today, he wouldn't do anything differently, although he'd worry much less. "It's daunting when you're young and the Empress was highly respected," he said. "Everyone was watching."[9]

With renovations well in hand, the Historic Area Society then set up a volunteer board, with one town council representative, to guide the theatre manager and staff. The Empress re-opened on March 3, 1989, with Juran Greene as manager and *Oliver and Company* on the screen. Greene had arrived in southern Alberta from Cleveland, Ohio the year before with a degree in drama (with an emphasis in theatre management). When he first drove past the Empress on a job-hunting safari, Art Ferrari and Al Park may well have been conferring below ground. Regardless, the theatre was closed, and Greene drove on. Less than a year later, he was hired to re-establish the theatre to a marquee attraction.

Because of previous difficulties, one of Greene's first jobs was convincing studios such as Disney and Warner Bros. to once again send films to the Empress. He called the studios and arranged to provide a $500 certified cheque to get the Empress back on the circuit.

As studios demanded a percentage of concession sales, Greene bought supplies wholesale from local distributors, lowering costs and keeping business within the town. Greene pushed the Empress board to allow the sale of wine and beer in the new basement and applied for the theatre's first liquor licence. He was vocal about the acts he wanted to bring in, not all of which met with board approval, but, according to Greene, produced profit for the theatre.[10]

The personal interests and perspectives of successive Empress managers have helped shape the fare and flavour offered on the theatre's stage. One might bring a love of Celtic and folk music, while another gives ascendency to blues, jazz and other genres. Classical music found its patron in Gerard Gibbs, an American who helped found the Fort Macleod International Music Festival in 2006. His personal friendship with Rivka Golani, a world-renowned violist, helped strengthen the festival which has survived his departure in 2010. Golani, a naturalized Canadian born in Israel, had played with the Israeli Philharmonic before moving to Canada in 1974 at age 28.[11] Golani used her star power and connections to draw major artists to the Empress.

In 2004, Golani, while a guest performer with the Edmonton symphony, was searching for remote locations to hold her master's workshops, says Denise Calderwood, former chair of the Empress board. Gibbs, an oboist also playing with the symphony, convinced Golani to consider the Empress as a possibility. "She was quite taken with the Empress when she saw it and agreed to come back. That was the beginning of the festival."[12] After the first couple of years, the event began to develop a wider interest, drawing up to 200 patrons to a classical music gathering in a small prairie town. To help defray costs, the Empress board obtained a grant from the Rural Alberta Development Fund to "grow and develop musical partnerships," says Calderwood. Some of those partnerships have taken word of the Empress venue to Japan, Venezuela, the United Kingdom, the United States and, of course, Israel.

Held the last weekend of May, the festival, in 2011, billeted 25 musicians in Fort Macleod, creating a tighter bond with the town, says Calderwood. A recent highlight has promoted southern Alberta to the world. British composer Benjamin Ellin, so taken with the Blackfoot history on a visit to the festival, composed two pieces commissioned by Golani: *Siksika* in 2010 and *Nahdoosi* in 2011. Both premiered at the festival and *Siksika* was performed in London, England in March 2011.

Catherine Ford, former *Calgary Herald* columnist, fan of the festival and frequent visitor to the Empress, reviewed the performance on her website:

> If it is possible for someone not of First Nations' ancestry, someone not of the Canadian landscape to capture the anticipation, sacred ritual, and excitement of the buffalo hunt, if it could be possible to outdo his evocative previous work [*Siksika*], Ellin has done so. When it was performed in the interpretive centre at Head-Smashed-In-Buffalo-Jump, on the very site where, since prehistoric times aboriginal hunters drove the buffalo to certain death and thus, food and fur for the winter, it was as if the piece, too, was part of this land and these people. At the climax of the piece, as the bass drum echoed off the stone, I had tears in my eyes.[13]

All the many positive aspects of the festival would likely never have accrued were it not for the Empress' ability to enchant Golani in 2004. Shawn Patience, Fort Macleod's mayor at this writing, agrees the theatre is a cornerstone of the community. "The Empress Theatre has, for a century, provided this community and region with entertainment opportunities that would likely have never been seen without the venerable theatre as a backdrop," says Patience. "Musical greats...come here to play because the theatre has a reputation that transcends its physical appearance, it has a mystique. Night after night, the Empress provides the historic streetscape with life as its well-known sign lights up the prairie evening and its doors open for those anxious to share in its charm."[14]

A succession of town councils has assisted the theatre financially, but the greatest support for the Empress is that shown by the people of Fort Macleod and area. "The Empress Theatre Society needs to be applauded for its efforts in continuing to provide Fort Macleod and all of southern Alberta with first-class entertainment," says Patience. "The combination of a beautiful, historic building and devoted individuals who are prepared to give of themselves ensures the great tradition of the Empress will continue long into its second century."[15]

Brent Hutchinson, manager as of this writing and a musician himself, has quickly come to understand the history in the brick and concrete. "You feel the presence of all those who have laughed and cried and squeezed hands in the Empress," says Hutchinson, a saxophonist whose tastes run to blues and jazz.[16] (He has played with a string of stars, including Muddy Waters, Joe Cocker and Stevie Ray Vaughn[17] and is a 2010 inductee of the VictoriaMusic Hall of Fame as a former member of Uncle Wiggly's Hot Shoes Blues Band, one of Victoria's first independent groups.) How many performers, wonders Hutchinson, have put on make-up in Empress dressing rooms while psyching themselves for waiting audiences? How many issues have been debated at town meetings here? How many local children have presented in a dance or piano recital?

Today, after a succession of managers each with their own vision for the Empress, the theatre remains a vital, vibrant part of community life in Fort Macleod, restored, yes, not as a museum but as a central character in the ongoing play of the town. That play, says David Coutts, honorary chairman of the Empress Theatre 2012 Centennial Committee, has produced a cast of well-known and highly regarded heroes, often cited in any history of the community, rough-and-ready souls in scarlet or buckskin who represent the romantic period of western pioneering. But, says Coutts, the area's MLA for 15 years (1993-2008), many of the visionaries and builders of the town, people who envisioned what Macleod could become and gambled on their beliefs, are less well known.

Giants such as James Lambert whose buildings have withstood time and functioned as intended for a century deserve, believes Coutts, the same recognition for their contributions as any pioneers. These heritage buildings, combined with the rich First Nations history of the area including Head-Smashed-In

> NIGHT AFTER NIGHT, THE EMPRESS PROVIDES THE HISTORIC STREETSCAPE WITH LIFE AS ITS WELL-KNOWN SIGN LIGHTS UP THE PRAIRIE EVENING AND ITS DOORS OPEN FOR THOSE ANXIOUS TO SHARE IN ITS CHARM.

Buffalo Jump, offered Fort Macleod something it could market to the world.

Although Coutts now lives in Edmonton, he still considers Fort Macleod home. Born in James Lambert's municipal hospital, Coutts has a soft spot for the builder's enduring gem, the Empress. It was, he recalls, his place on Saturday afternoons, while during the rest of the week he watched the airmen his mother took in as boarders head to the Empress for their fill of entertainment. He acted in several Playgoers' presentations, directed *Steel Magnolias*, and took a turn in one of the summer theatre performances, *Big Sky*, playing a town mayor. He served on the Historic Area Society before entering provincial politics, placing him at the rebirth of the Empress in the 1980s.

"The community looks at the Empress as a wonderful icon that seems to transcend time," says Coutts. "It has come to represent what the community has gone through during the last 100 years. It brought the town news of the Second World War, suffered through the doldrums in the early days of television, and has survived everything to give people a chance to see live performances. It has been the constant. I can still smell Dan Boyle's cigar and see his red usher's flashlight. He'd stand at the end of the corridor and tear your ticket in half and smile at you. You knew you were in."

Coutts, who took his children to see *Star Wars* in the theatre he once sat in as a child, compares the relatively young Empress to the castles and cathedrals of Europe; the difference, he says, at least for him: the Empress is home. It's a favourite southern Alberta place for Coutts, along with two others that many readers will have shared.

One is standing on the cliff at Head-Smashed-In Buffalo Jump, drinking in the panorama from 72 individual mountain peaks to green, rolling foothills and, through 180 degrees, the platter-flat landscape to the east. The vista, he says, shows the wonders of southwestern Alberta, and to him represents life.

The second is much less sweeping but no less inspiring. Standing at the back of the Empress stage, out of the limelight, the viewer can see everything going on in the theatre in that moment: the reaction of the audience, the players on stage, the performers preparing in the wings for their chance to go on. It is, he says, the definition of solitude. Coutts says the resolve of Fort Macleod citizens to keep the Empress strong ensures her reign will extend into the next 100 years. It is an act of faith, of keeping unbroken the town's link with its past. The Empress, he says, will entertain generations to come.

"That building," says Coutts, "won't ever let them down."[18]

APPENDIX

## Owners of the Empress Theatre, 1912-present
Source: Service Alberta/Land Titles, Calgary

| | |
|---|---|
| Thomas B. Martin | 1912 – August 25, 1928 |
| Ruby G. Martin | August 25, 1928 – November 13, 1928 |
| Augustus T. Leather | November 13, 1928 (2:48 p.m.) |
| James A. Booth and William E. Beatty | November 13, 1928 (2:49 p.m.) – June 26, 1929 |
| James A. Booth and Cecil J. Hughes | June 26, 1929 – November 4, 1931 |
| Augustus T. Leather | November 4, 1931 – March 30, 1932 |
| British Canadian Trust Co. | March 30, 1932 – August 25, 1932 |
| Augustus T. Leather | August 25, 1932 – March 27, 1934 |
| Jessie G. Leather | March 27, 1934 – January 11, 1937 |
| Daniel A. Boyle | January 11, 1937 – September 18, 1963 |
| M. Edna Boyle | September 18, 1963 – October 1, 1963 |
| Richard V. Kiefer | October 1, 1963 – May 16, 1973 |
| Gerardus A. Goedhart | May 16, 1973 – November 8, 1977 |
| Centre Cinemas Ltd. | November 8, 1977 – November 8, 1977 |
| Larry B. Becker | November 8, 1977 – January 27, 1982 |
| Suresh B. Prasad and Sylvana La Selva | January 27, 1982 – September 26, 1986 |
| Suresh B. Prasad | September 26, 1986 – April 24, 1987 |
| Fort Macleod Provincial Historic Area Society | April 24, 1987 – May 14, 1990 |
| Town of Fort Macleod | May 14, 1990 – present |

END NOTES

**CHAPTER 1**

[1] *Los Angeles Herald*, April 8, 1907. Retrieved from http://chroniclingamerica.loc.gov/lccn/sn85042462/1907-04-08/ed-1/seq-1/.

[2] http://www.ebay.com/itm/Mysterious-MR-Raffles-ad-Chicago-IL-Postcard-/160604114751.

**CHAPTER 2**

[1] *The Macleod Advertiser,* January 18, 1912.

[2] Judy Rennie interview, October 15, 2011.

[3] Ibid., October 15, 2011.

[4] Judy Rennie and David Rennie, *Old Man's River*, p. 72.

[5] Richard B. Nevitt, *A Winter at Fort Macleod*, ed. Hugh Dempsey, p.33.

[6] Ibid., p. 119.

[7] Visiting Fort Macleod, www.fortmacleod.com/visiting/attractions/Main%20Street%20History.cfm.

[8] History of Fort Macleod, An Overview, www.fortmacleod.com/visiting/history/default.cfm.

[9] Rise M. Massey, "The Empress Theatre," Paper prepared for Alberta Culture, 1981, p. 2.

[10] Frontier Opera Houses, Encyclopedia of the Great Plains, http://plainshumanities.unl.edu/encyclopedia/doc/egp.mus.018.

[11] *The Macleod Advertiser,* January 23, January 30, February 8, 1912.

[12] Ibid., January 18, 1912.

[13] Ibid., February 8, 1912.

[14] Ibid., February 22, 1912.

[15] Ibid., January 18, 1912.

[16] Ibid., January 18, 1912.

**CHAPTER 3**

[1] Archibald Oswald MacRae, *History of the Province of Alberta*, The Western Canadian History Co., 1912.

[2] Beaux-Arts Architecture, http://en.wikipedia.org/wiki/Beaux-Arts_architecture.

[3] World's Columbian Exposition, http://en.wikipedia.org/wiki/World%27s_Columbian_Exposition.

[4] Beaux-Arts Architecture, http://en.wikipedia.org/wiki/Beaux-Arts_architecture#Beaux-Arts_in_Canada.

[5] *Fort Macleod – Our Colourful Past: A History of the Town of Fort Macleod from 1874-1924*, p. 340.

[6] Marselle Jobs Thompson, "The Empress Theatre in Fort Macleod, Alberta," M.A. dissertation U of A, 1990, p. 23-26.

[7] Donald Wetherell and Irene Kmet, *Town Life*, p. 222.

[8] *The Macleod Spectator*, October 8, 1912.

[9] Donald Wetherell and Irene Kmet, *Town Life*, p. 175.

[10] *The Macleod Advertiser*, February 1, 1912.

[11] Ibid., March 14, 1912.

[12] Ibid., , May 16, 1912.

[13] *The Macleod Spectator*, June 4, 1912.

[14] *The Macleod Advertiser*, June 6, 1912.

[15] Ibid., June 13, 1912.

[16] Ibid., June 13, 1912.

[17] Ibid., July 4, 1912.

[18] Marselle Jobs Thompson, "The Empress Theatre in Fort Macleod, Alberta," M.A. dissertation U of A, 1990, p.41.

[19] *The Macleod Spectator*, August 13, 1912.

**CHAPTER 4**

[1] *The Macleod Spectator*, December 31, 1912.

[2] Ibid., October 23, 1912.

[3] The Pollards, http://homepages.paradise.net.nz/polopera/.

[4] Stephen E. Busch, Juvenile Opera Companies, www.operaoldcolo.info/personages/company7.html.

[5] Paul Gilmore, http://en.wikipedia.org/wiki/Paul_Gilmore.

[6] Marselle Jobs Thompson, "The Empress Theatre in Fort Macleod, Alberta," M.A. dissertation U of A, 1990, p. 50.

[7] *The Macleod Spectator*, May 28, 1914.

## END NOTES

8 Ibid., August 6, 1914.
9 Minstrel Show, http://en.wikipedia.org/wiki/Minstrel_show.
10 *The Macleod Spectator*, December 31, 1914.
11 Ibid., January 21, 1915.
12 Ibid., August 15, 1915.
13 Ibid., October 14, 1915.
14 Ibid., November 4, 1915.
15 Ibid., February 24, 1916.
16 Ibid., March 23, 1916.
17 Ibid., May 25, 1916.
18 Ibid., June 29, 1916.

**CHAPTER 5**

1 *The Macleod Spectator*, July 6, 1916.
2 Ibid., August 3, 1916.
3 *The Macleod News*, November 30, 1916.
4 Ibid., December 7, 1916.
5 Charles Urban, Motion Picture Pioneer www.charlesurban.com/.
6 Charles Urban, Motion Picture Pioneer, www.charlesurban.com/war.htm.
7 *The Macleod News*, December 15, 1916.
8 Ibid., January 4, 1917.
9 Ibid., January 4, 1917.
10 Ibid., November 1, 1917.
11 Marselle Jobs Thompson, "The Empress Theatre in Fort Macleod, Alberta," pp. 61-62.
12 Dennis James interview, November 11, 2010.
13 Daisy Young interview, November 20, 2010.
14 *Fort Macleod – Our Colourful Past*, p. 47.
15 *The Macleod News*, November 28, 1918.
16 *Fort Macleod – Our Colourful Past*, p. 47.
17 The Unpardonable Sin (1919), www.imdb.com/title/tt0010825/.
18 *The Macleod News*, July 17, 1919.
19 Ibid., October 9, 1919.
20 Ibid., November 29, 1919.
21 Ibid., November 13, 1919.

22 Ibid., June 30, 1920.
23 Ibid., January 31, 1918.
24 Brief Bio of Vaudeville, http://tribes.tribe.net/blankerslate/thread/44516aa9-06f9-4875-afb8-d94550f3f498.
25 *The Macleod News*, November 14, 1929.
26 Gold Diggers of Broadway, http://en.wikipedia.org/wiki/Gold_Diggers_of_Broadway.
27 Marselle Jobs Thompson, "The Empress Theatre in Fort Macleod, Alberta," M.A. dissertation U of A, 1990, p. 67.
28 *The Macleod News*, April 1, 1920.

**CHAPTER 6**

1 Marselle Jobs Thompson, "The Empress Theatre in Fort Macleod, Alberta," M.A. dissertation U of A, 1990, p. 69
2 *Fort Macleod – Our Colourful Past: A History of the Town of Fort Macleod from 1874-1924*, p. 205.
3 Ibid., p. 32.
4 Ibid., p. 45.
5 *The Macleod Times*, October 11, 1928.
6 Ibid., November 8, 1928.
7 Ibid., November 29, 1928.
8 Ibid., June 27, 1929.
9 Ibid., November 7, 1929.
10 Ibid., November 7, 1929.
11 Ibid., March 27, 1930.
12 Ibid., October 23, 1930.
13 *The Macleod Gazette*, March 19, 1931.
14 Ibid., May 28, 1931.
15 Ibid., September 3, 1931.
16 Ibid., November 17, 1931.
17 Ibid., November 17, 1931.
18 Ibid., January 7, 1932.
19 Abel Green and Joe Laurie Jr., *Show Biz from Vaude to Video*.
20 *The Macleod Gazette*, May 19, 1932.
21 Ibid., August 25, 1932.

END NOTES

22  Ibid., October 20, 1932.
23  Ibid., September 13, 1934.
24  Ibid., May 2, 1935.

**CHAPTER 7**

1  *Leavings by Trail – Granum by Rail*, pp. 189-191.
2  Mary Yvonne Dunne, "Dan Boyle and the Empress Theatre: A Motion Picture Pioneer Story," Unpublished manuscript.
3  Ibid.
4  Ibid.
5  Ibid.
6  Ibid.
7  Ibid.
8  Ibid.
9  Ibid.
10  Ibid.
11  Ibid.
12  Ibid.
13  Ibid.
14  Ronald. W. Clay, "*The History of the Fort Macleod Empress Theatre*," p. 9.
15  Juran Greene interview, August 9, 2011.
16  Rod Cameron – biography, www.imdb.com/name/nm0131713/bio.
17  *Fort Macleod – Our Colourful Past II*, p. 302.
18  Bill Thompson, http://en.wikipedia.org/wiki/Bill_Thompson_(voice_actor).
19  Mary Yvonne Dunne, "Dan Boyle and the Empress Theatre: A Motion Picture Pioneer Story," Unpublished manuscript.
20  Ibid.
21  Glenbow Archives, Empress Theatre Collection.
22  Snow White, http://en.wikipedia.org/wiki/Snow_White_and_the_Seven_Dwarfs_%281937_film%29.
23  Mary Ruller interview, January 21, 2011.
24  Glenbow Archives, Empress Theatre Collection.
25  Ibid.
26  Ibid.

**CHAPTER 8**

1  Glenbow Archives, Empress Theatre Collection.
2  Ibid.
3  Ibid.
4  Ibid.
5  Mary Yvonne Dunne, "Dan Boyle and the Empress Theatre: A Motion Picture Pioneer Story," Unpublished manuscript.
6  Ibid.
7  Ibid.
8  Ibid.
9  Ibid.
10  The Fine Art of Neil Boyle and Betty Boyle, www.neilboyle.com.
11  Today's Inspiration, http://todaysinspiration.blogspot.com/search?q=boyle.
12  Bob Hart and Ken Hart interview, January 21, 2011.
13  Today's Inspiration, http://todaysinspiration.blogspot.com/search?q=boyle.
14  Bonnie Kennedy, "Artist Neil Boyle: One of Southern Alberta's Own," *Lethbridge living*, p. 73.
15  Betty Boyle interview, April 16, 2011.

**CHAPTER 9**

1  Darrel Fraser interview, November 20, 2010.
2  Edith Becker interview, July 23, 2011.
3  *The Macleod Gazette*, November 10, 1979.
4  Delle Schmidt interview, November 17, 2011.
5  Edith Becker interview, July 23, 2011.
6  Melanie Fast, "Spirits of Southern Alberta," *Expressions*, 2008, p. 38.
7  Sharon Hellman interview, January 21, 2011.
8  Ryland Moranz interview, November 5, 2010.
9  Juran Greene interview, August 9, 2011.
10  Dean Poetz, "Ghostly atmosphere developing at Empress," *The Macleod Gazette*, April 1, 1992.
11  Juran Greene interview, August 9, 2011.

**END NOTES**

**CHAPTER 10**

1   Main Street Project History, www.fortmacleod.com.

2   Jim Mountain interview, June 26, 2011.

3   Louise Heric and Sharon Monical interview, February 23, 2011.

4   George Mann, *Theatre Lethbridge: A History of Theatrical Production in Lethbridge, Alberta (1885 – 1988)*, p. 231.

5   Ibid., pg 231.

6   Ibid., pg 231.

7   Wes Olmstead interview, September 15, 2011.

8   Al Park interview, August 10, 2011.

9   Art Ferrari interview, May 17, 2011.

10   Juran Greene interview, August 9, 2011.

11   Rivka Golani – Viola, www.thecanadianencyclopedia.com/index.cfm?PgNm=TCE&Params=U1ARTU0001391.

12   Denise Calderwood interview, October 5, 2011.

13   Macleod International Music Festival – Priceless, www.troymedia.com/2011/06/05/fort-macleod-international-music-festival-priceless/.

14   Shawn Patience interview, October 13, 2011.

15   Ibid., October 13, 2011.

16   Brent Hutchinson interview, January 21, 2011.

17   Hornby Island Blues Workshop, www.hornby-blues.bc.ca/instructors/brenthutchinson/.

18   Dave Coutts interview, September 21, 2011.

**REFERENCES**

## Books, Articles and Archival Sources

Clay, Ronald. W. "The History of the Fort Macleod Empress Theatre." Paper prepared for Main Street Fort Macleod, March 1989.

Downes, Peter. *The Pollards.* Wellington, N.Z.: Steele Roberts Publishing, 2002.

Dunne, Mary Yvonne. "Dan Boyle and the Empress Theatre: A Motion Picture Pioneer." Unpublished manuscript.

Fast, Melanie. "Spirits of Southern Alberta," *Expressions*, April 2008.

*Fort Macleod – Our Colourful Past: A history of the town of Fort Macleod from 1874 to 1924.* Fort Macleod, Alberta: Fort Macleod History Book Committee, 1977.

*Fort Macleod – Our Colourful Past II: A History of Fort Macleod and District 1925 to 1989.* Fort Macleod, Alberta: Fort Macleod History Book Committee, 1990.

Glenbow Archives, Empress Theatre Collection.

Green, Abel and Laurie Jr., Joe. *Show Biz from Vaude to Video.* N.p.: Holt, 1951.

*Leavings by Trail – Granum by Rail.* Granum, Alberta: Granum History Committee, 1979.

Jobs Thompson, Marselle. "The Empress Theatre in Fort Macleod, Alberta." M.A. dissertation, University of Alberta, 1990.

Kennedy, Bonnie. "Artist Neil Boyle: One of Southern Alberta's Own." *Lethbridge living*, spring 2006.

MacRae, Archibald Oswald. History of the Province of Alberta. Edmonton: The Western Canadian History Co., 1912.

Mann, George. *Theatre Lethbridge: A History of Theatrical Production in Lethbridge, Alberta (1885 – 1988).* Calgary: Detsileg Enterprises Ltd., 1993.

Massey, Rise M. "The Empress Theatre." Paper prepared for Alberta Culture, Historical Resources, Historic Site Service, 1981.

Nevitt, Richard B., *A Winter at Fort Macleod*, ed. Hugh Dempsey. N.p.: Glenbow Alberta Institute/McClelland Stewart West, 1974.

Poetz, Dean. "Ghostly atmosphere developing at Empress." *The Macleod Gazette,* April 1, 1992.

Rennie, Judy L. and Rennie, David L. Old Man's River. Toronto: n.p., 2008.

Watkins, Mel. *On the Real Side: Laughing, Lying, and Signifying—The Underground Tradition of African-American Humor that Transformed American Culture, from Slavery to Richard Pryor.* New York: Simon & Schuster, 1994.

Wetherell, Donald G. and Kmet, Irene R. A. *Town Life: Main Street and the Evolution of Small Town Alberta,* 1880-1947. Edmonton: University of Alberta Press, 1995.

REFERENCES

## Historic Newspapers

*The Macleod Advertiser*

*The Macleod Gazette*

*The Macleod News*

*The Macleod Spectator*

*The Macleod Times*

*The newspapers listed above provided much of what is known about the earliest history of the Empress Theatre. The University of Lethbridge Library has begun digitizing historic newspapers for the library's Southern Alberta Newspaper Collection. The digitized issues may be accessed at www.uleth.ca/lib/digitzed_Collections/sanews.asp.

## Websites

Beaux-Arts Architecture,http://en.wikipedia.org/wiki/Beaux-Arts_architecture.

Beaux-Arts Architecture, http://en.wikipedia.org/wiki/Beaux-Arts_architecture#Beaux-Arts_in_Canada

Blackface, http://en.wikipedia.org/wiki/Minstrel_show#CITEREFWatkins1994http://en.wikipedia.org/wiki/Minstrel_show.

Brief Bio of Vaudeville, tribes.tribe.net/blankerslate/thread/44516aa9-06f9-4875-afb8-d94550f3f498.

Britain Prepared, filmreference.com.

Stephen E. Busch, Juvenile Opera Companies. www.operaoldcolo.info/personages/company7.html.

Rod Cameron – biography, www.imdb.com/name/nm0131713/bio.

eBay: www.ebay.com/itm/Mysterious-MR-Raffles-ad-Chicago-IL-Postcard-/160604114751.

The Fine Art of Neil Boyle and Betty Boyle, www.neilboyle.com.

Frontier Opera Houses, Encyclopedia of the Great Plains,http://plainshumanities.unl.edu/encyclopedia/doc/egp.mus.018.

Catherine Ford, Macleod International Music Festival – Priceless, www.troymedia.com/2011/06/05/fort-macleod-international-music-festival-priceless/.

Paul Gilmore, http://en.wikipedia.org/wiki/Paul_Gilmore.

Rivka Golani – Viola, www.thecanadianencyclopedia.com/index.cfm?PgNm=TCE&Params=U1ARTU0001391.

Gold Diggers of Broadway, http://en.wikipedia.org/wiki/Gold_Diggers_of_Broadway.

History of Fort Macleod – An Overview, www.fortmacleod.com/visiting/history/default.cfm.

Hornby Island Blues Workshop – biography for Brent Hutchinson, www.hornby-blues.bc.ca/instructors/brenthutchinson/.

Los Angeles Herald, April 8, 1907, chroniclingamerica.loc.gov/lccn/sn85042462/1907-04-08/ed-1/seq-1/.

Main Street Project History, www.fortmacleod.com.

Minstrel Show, http://en.wikipedia.org/wiki/Minstrel_show#CITEREFWatkins1994http://en.wikipedia.org/wiki/Minstrel_show.

The Pollards, http://homepages.paradise.net.nz/polopera/.

Snow White, http://en.wikipedia.org/wiki/Snow_White_and_the_Seven_Dwarfs_%281937_film%29

Bill Thompson, http://en.wikipedia.org/wiki/Bill_Thompson_(voice_actor).

Today's Inspiration, todaysinspiration.blogspot.com/search?q=boyle.

The Unpardonable Sin, www.imdb.com/title/tt0010825/.

Charles Urban – Motion Picture Pioneer, www.charlesurban.com/.

Charles Urban – Motion Picture Pioneer, www.charlesurban.com/war.htm.

World's Columbian Exposition, http://en.wikipedia.org/wiki/World%27s_Columbian_Exposition.

**REFERENCES**

## Interviews

Becker, Edith, interviewed July 23, 2011.

Boyle, Betty, interviewed April 16, 2011.

Calderwood, Denise, interviewed October 5, 2011.

Coutts, Dave interviewed September 21, 2011.

Ferrari, Art, interviewed May 17, 2011.

Fraser, Darrel, interviewed November 20, 2010.

Greene, Juran, interviewed August 9, 2011.

Hart, Bob and Hart, Ken, interviewed January 21, 2011.

Hellman, Sharon, interviewed January 21, 2011.

Heric, Louise and Monical, Sharon, interviewed February 23, 2011.

Hutchinson, Brent, interviewed January 21, 2011.

James, Dennis, interviewed November 11, 2010.

Moranz, Ryland, interviewed November 5, 2010.

Mountain, Jim, interviewed June 26, 2011.

Olmstead, Wes, interviewed September 15, 2011.

Park, Al, interviewed August 10, 2011.

Patience, Shawn interviewed October 13, 2011.

Rennie, Judy, interviewed October 15, 2011.

Ruller, Mary, interviewed January 21, 2011.

Schmidt, Delle, interviewed November 17, 2011.

Young, Daisy, interviewed November 20, 2010.

## Author

Photo: Christina Boese

Peter J. Scott spent 30 years in daily newspapers throughout Western Canada as a reporter and editor. Born in England and raised in Regina, Saskatchewan, he now lives and works near Lethbridge, Alberta as a freelance writer, journalist and educator.

# INDEX